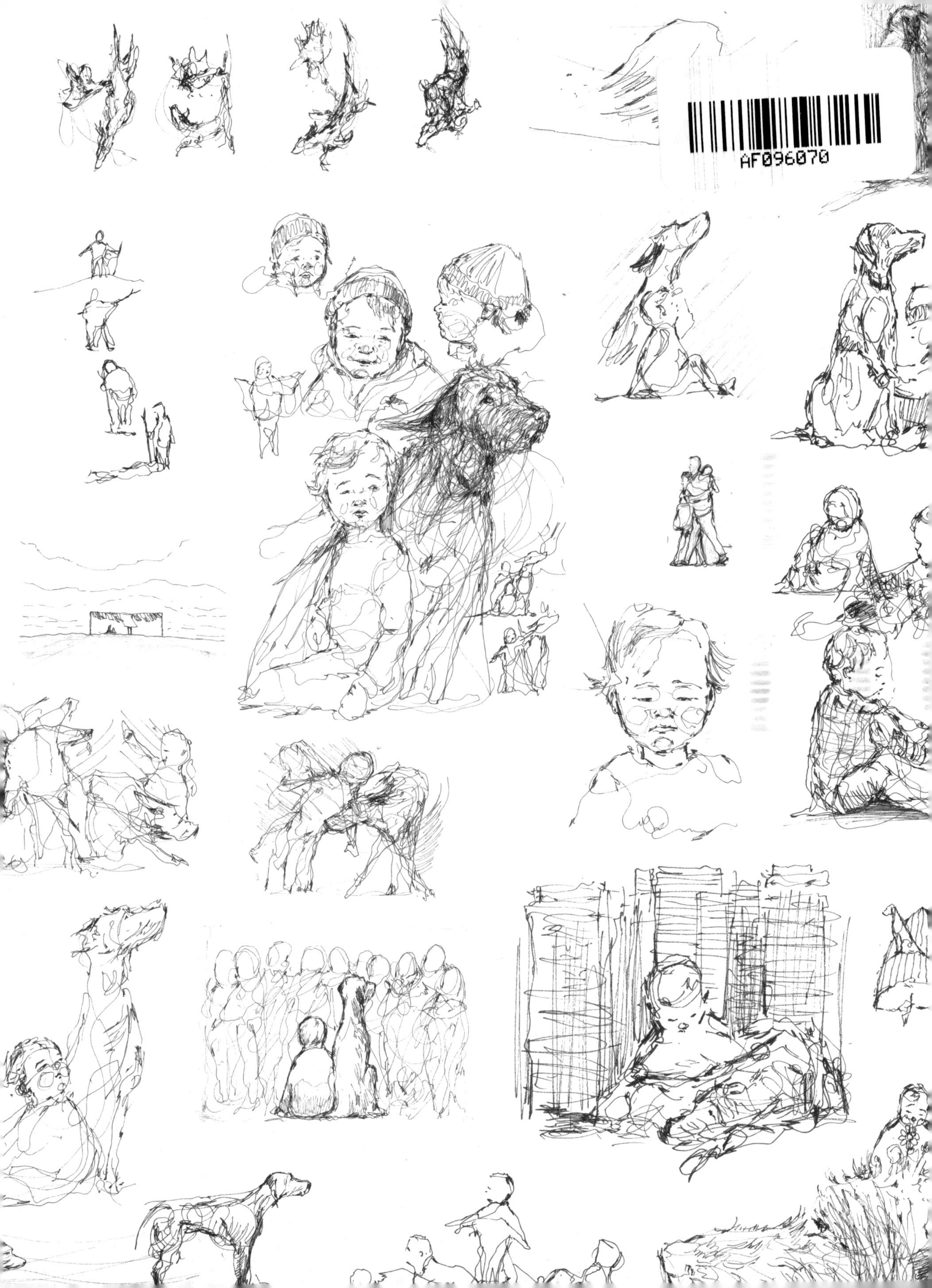

To Those Who Speak

A Message of Love from Father to Son

From the *Sunday Times* bestselling author
Luke Adam Hawker

*This book is for anyone who speaks
without words, and for all those
who are willing to listen.*

Foreword

This book is a testament to the power of communication beyond words. I hope it inspires people to listen more, and to connect with the unspoken conversations happening all around us.

I think it's important to be honest with you that I am writing this book backwards. That is to say, as I write these words, each and every drawing in the book is already complete and (in my view) is exactly where it needs to be. The words have come afterwards. This is not a conventional way to create a book, but it is the way that feels truest to me as an artist. I have always thought better in pictures. When words fail me, as they often do, images come.

In a way, this book is an invitation: a challenge to read in a way that you perhaps haven't before. This book could be read in about five minutes, if you only read the words. But you won't see all there is to be seen unless you truly take the time to look. So much of what I'm saying is embedded in the artworks.

This is not a children's book, but it is not *not* a children's book. It is full of moments of struggle, joy, pain, dread, relief and reflection. It spans an almost five-year period, at the start of which my son Harry was born, and my wife Lizzie and I began our life with him as a family. We knew Harry was unique from birth. He has an extra X chromosome, making him XXY. He is also non-verbal, and, now aged almost five, he hasn't ticked all the boxes or hit the developmental milestones that children are expected to. He is particularly susceptible to respiratory issues, and it was this that ended up taking him into hospital at a very young age. It was the scariest time of our lives, and there were moments when we didn't know whether we would be able to take him home. This book tells the story of Harry's first few years, including this period: the highs and the lows, the fear and pain, and most importantly, the power of love to pull us through it all.

As parents, we have been on a journey for answers that has only led us to more questions. There was a time I was so wrapped up in finding out why Harry was different, that I was missing the beauty that was held in those differences. As a parent, I assumed it was my job to have all the answers, to teach my child to understand. I now realise that the lessons have been mine to learn.

Harry has shown me that non-verbal communication is in fact our most universal and shared mother tongue, linking us all with one another, and the natural world around us. It has been a great source of joy for me to watch his deep kinship with our family dog, Robin, blossom – a bond that is at the heart of this book.

Harry has taught me so much, from everyday realisations to core simple truths. That pride is born from your efforts, not results. That the things you can't do can have as much of a positive impact on your life as the things you can. That listening to one another goes beyond what you can hear with your ears. That seeing requires more than good eyesight. And that when we pause to truly listen, everything speaks.

My son has taught me more without words than every spoken conversation of my life so far. This book is my expression of gratitude to him for this invaluable education.

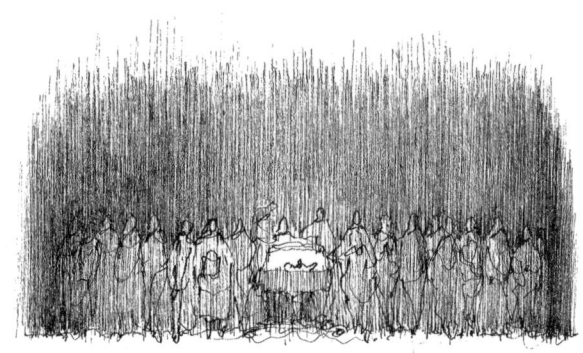

Everyone wondered when you would talk.
You patiently waited for us to listen.

Then came the forms to fill in, each tick-box
left empty.

We were told you were delayed.
But it was the world that was
rushing around you.

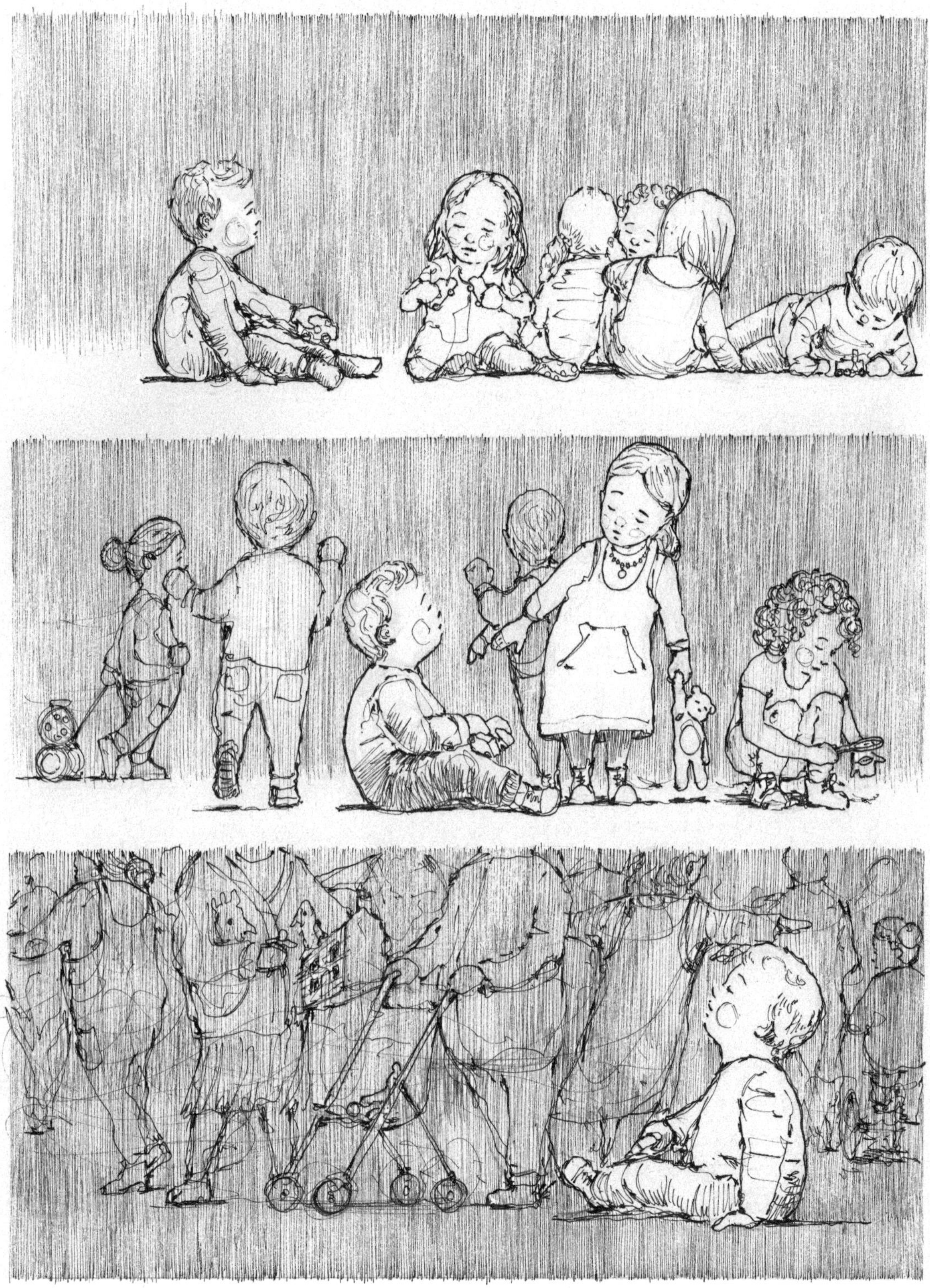

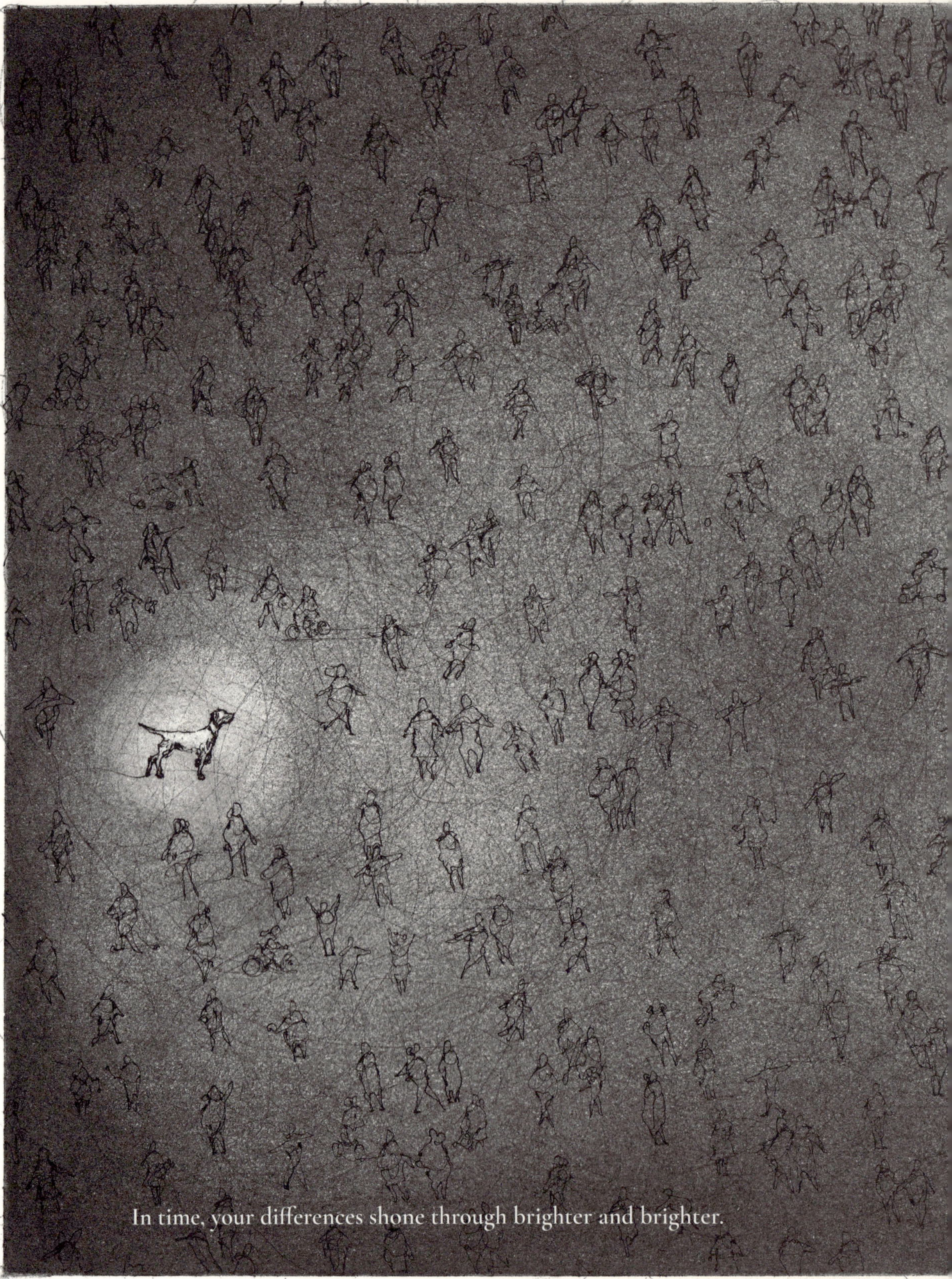
In time, your differences shone through brighter and brighter.

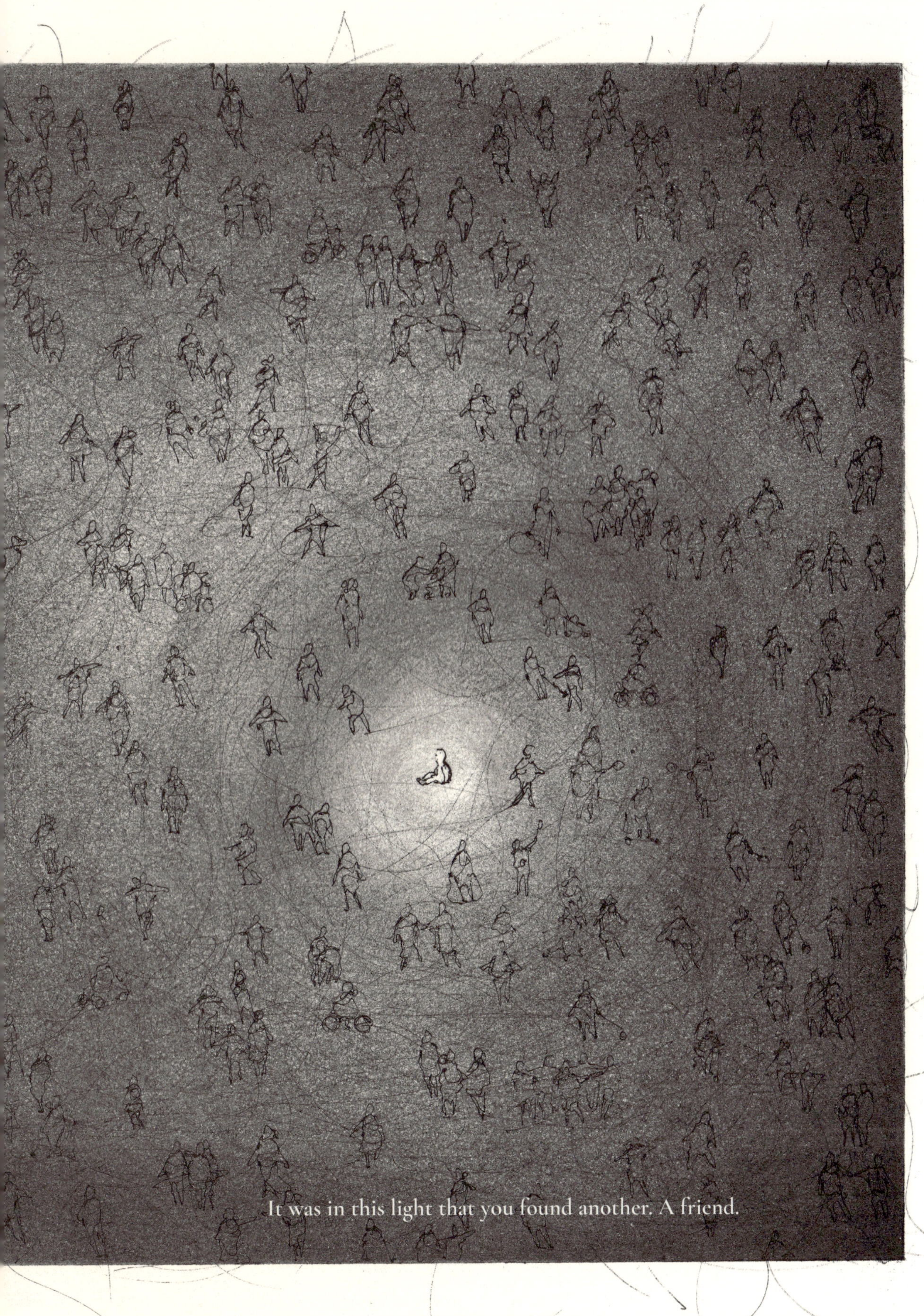
It was in this light that you found another. A friend.

You shared an unspoken language.

Silence needn't mean solitude.

You gave us a glimpse of a universal conversation
unfolding all around us.

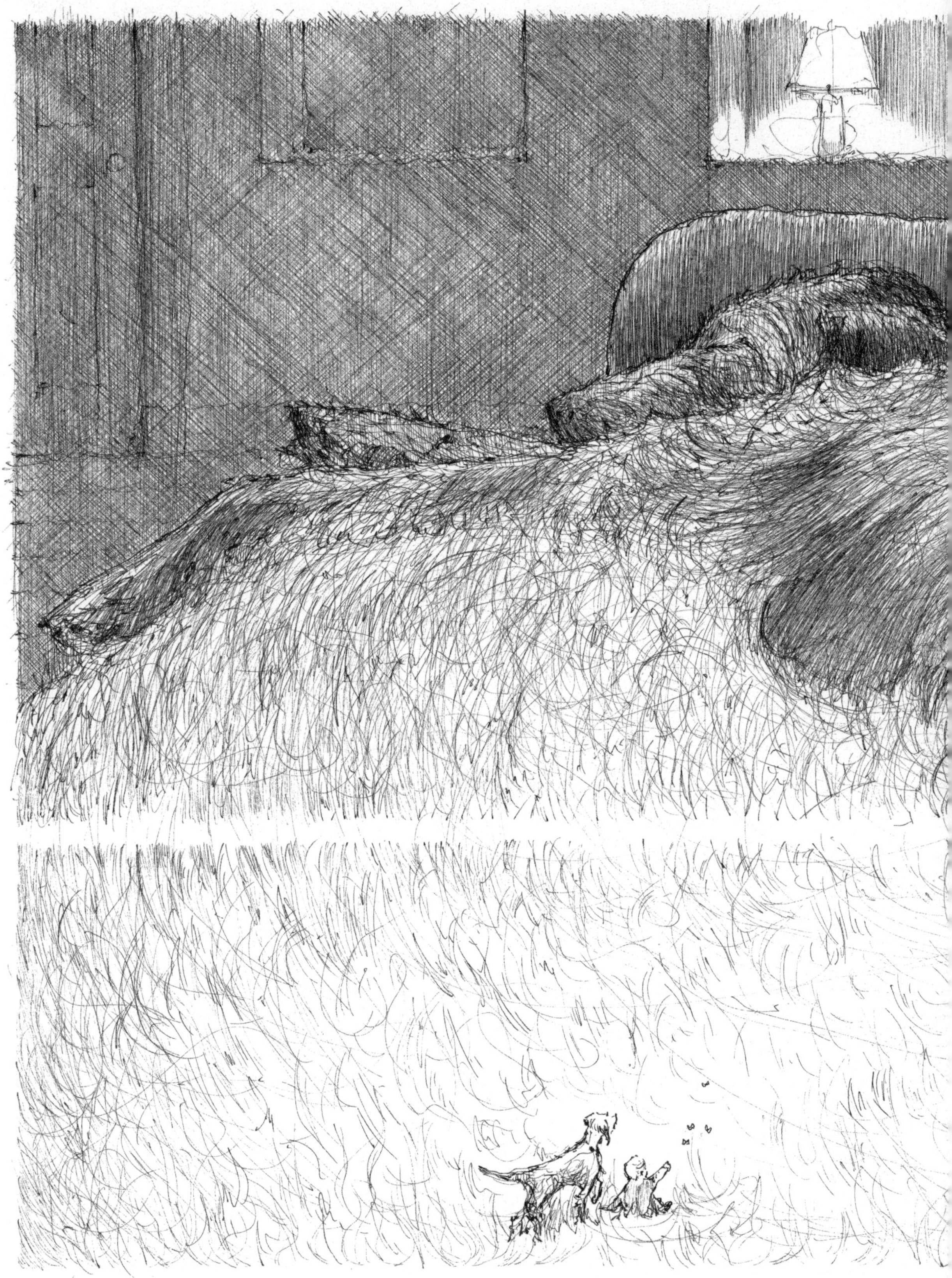

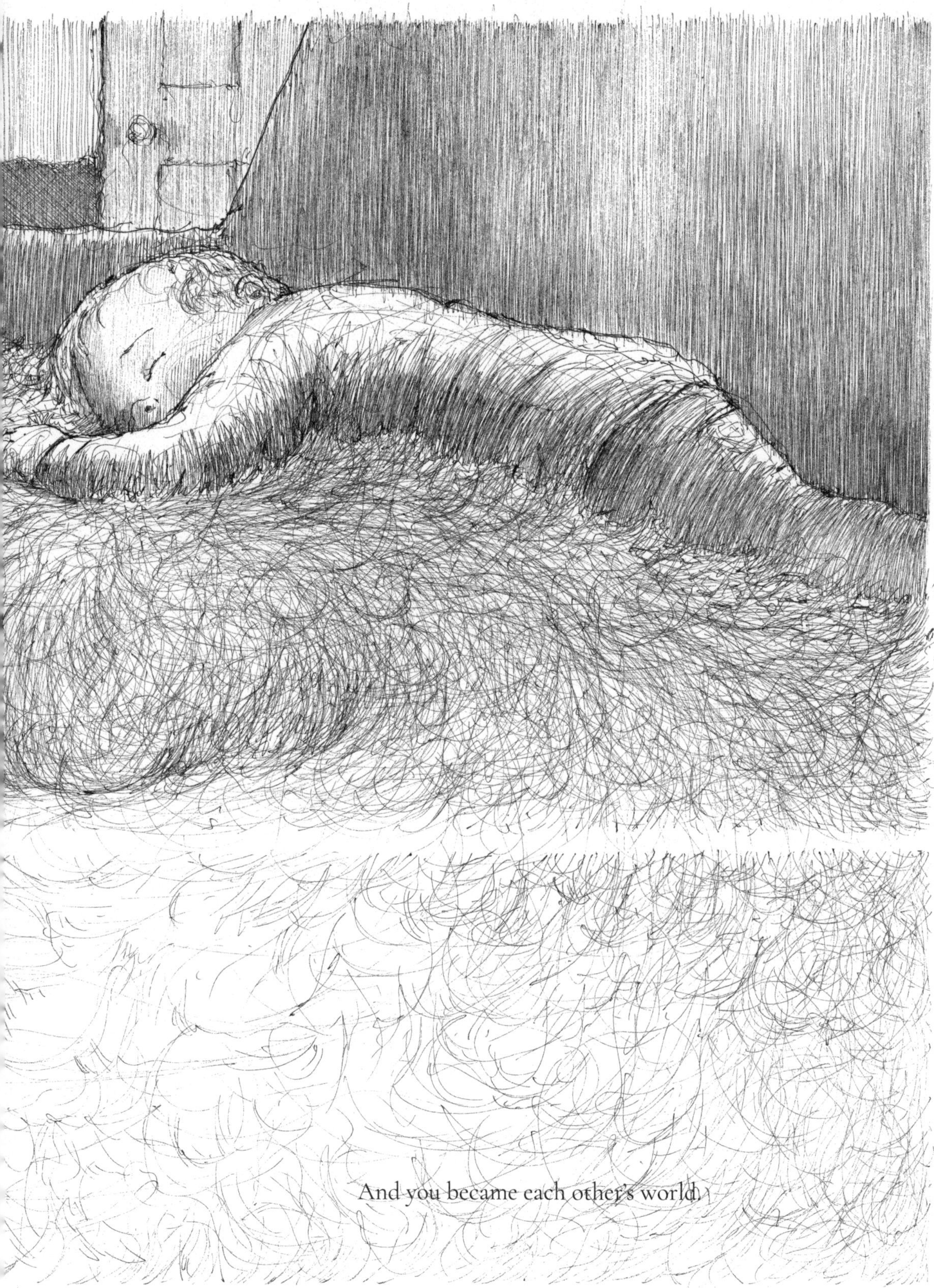

And you became each other's world.

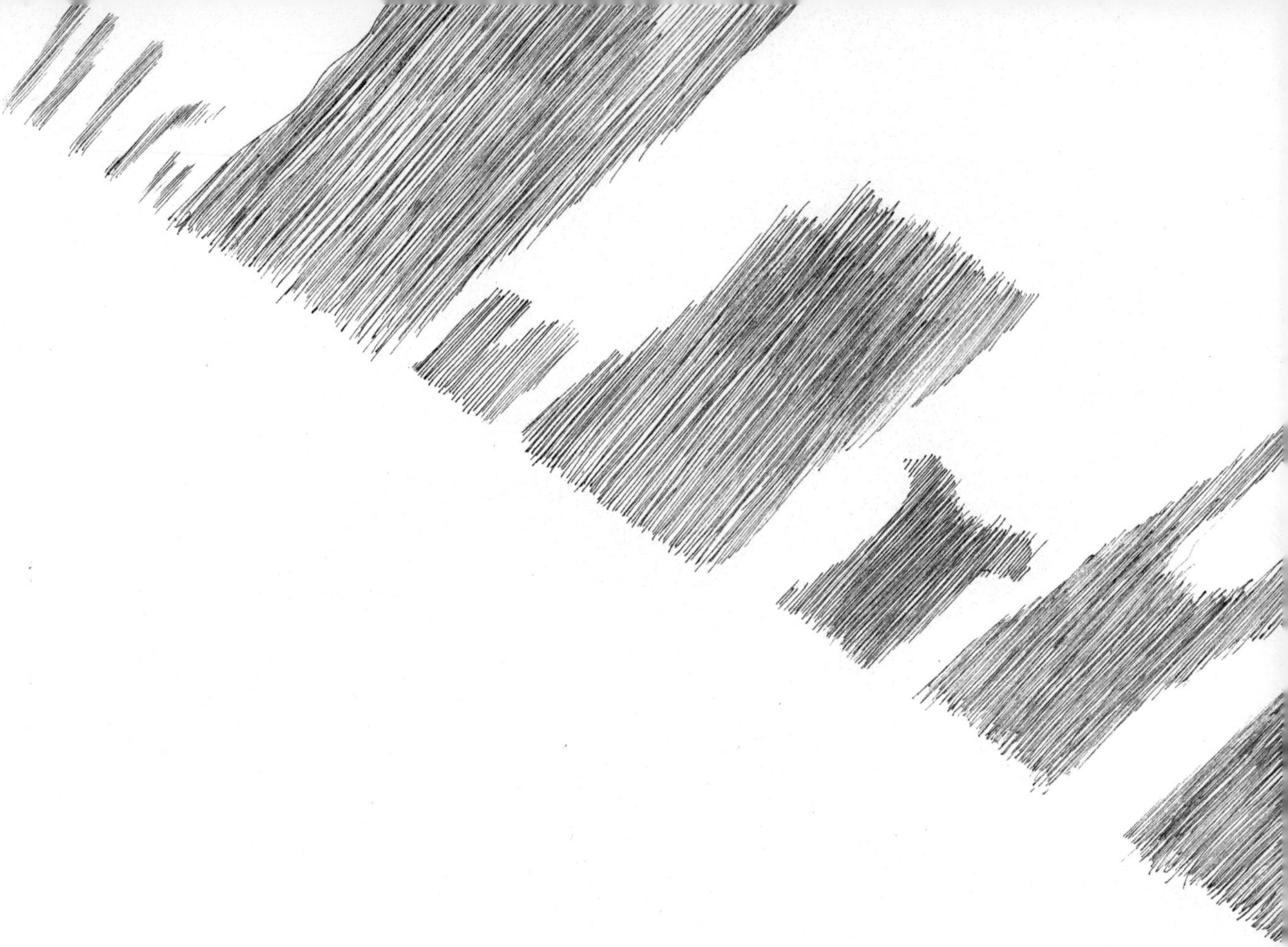

Inseparable, you grew together.

Seeing differently,
feeling differently.

You showed us the beauty of irregularities.

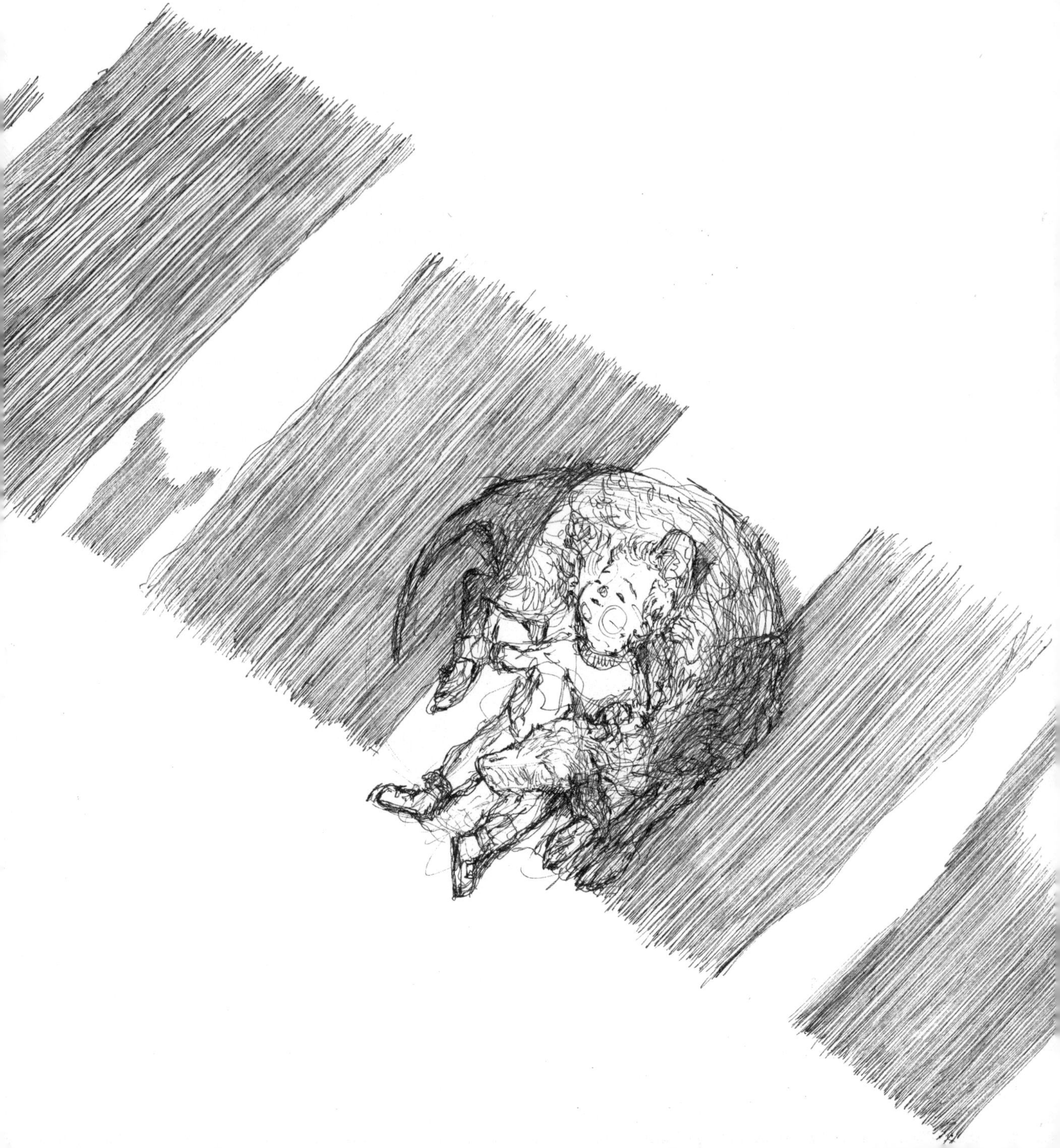

You began to find your melody,
humming to your own tune.

Our songbird.

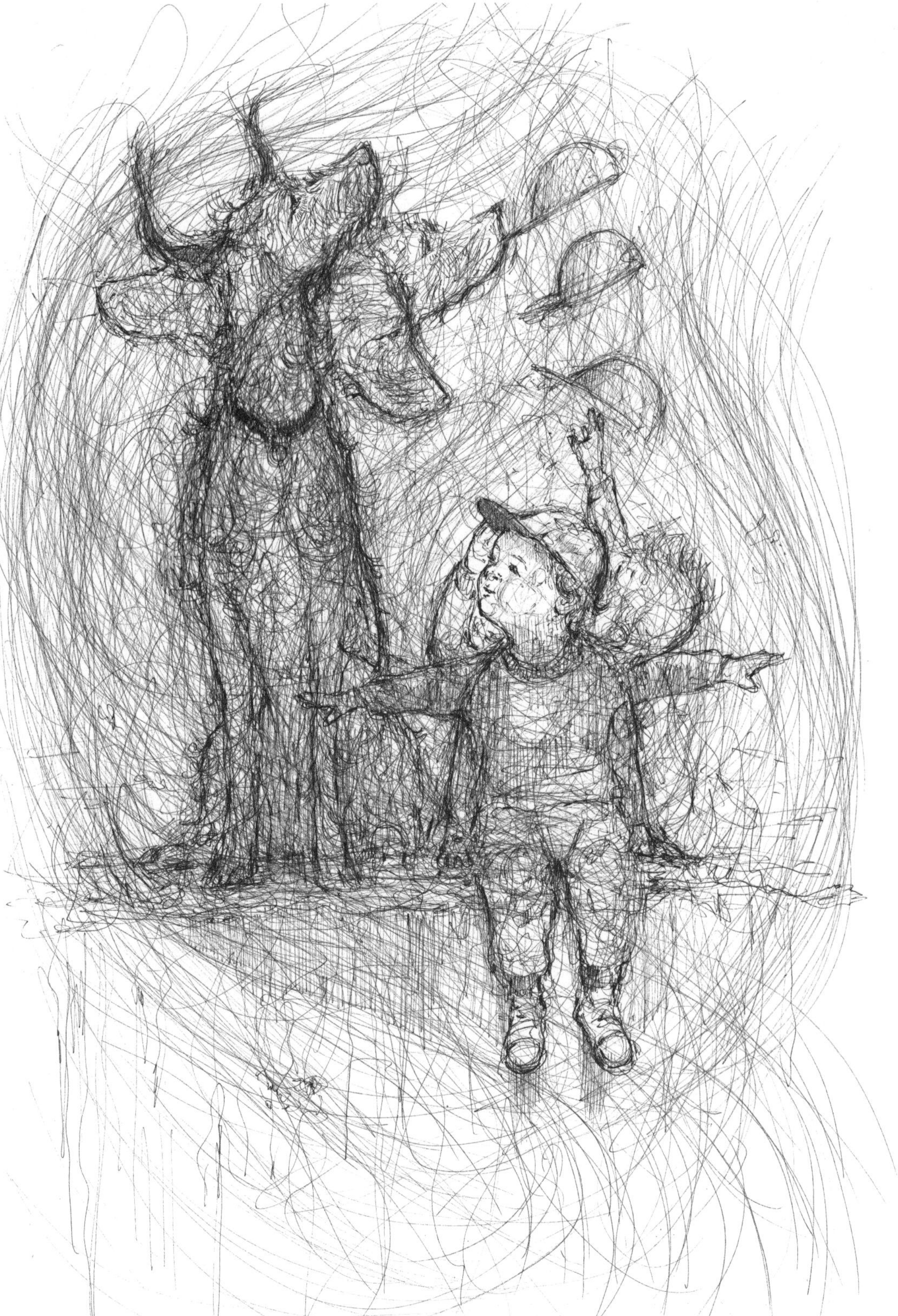

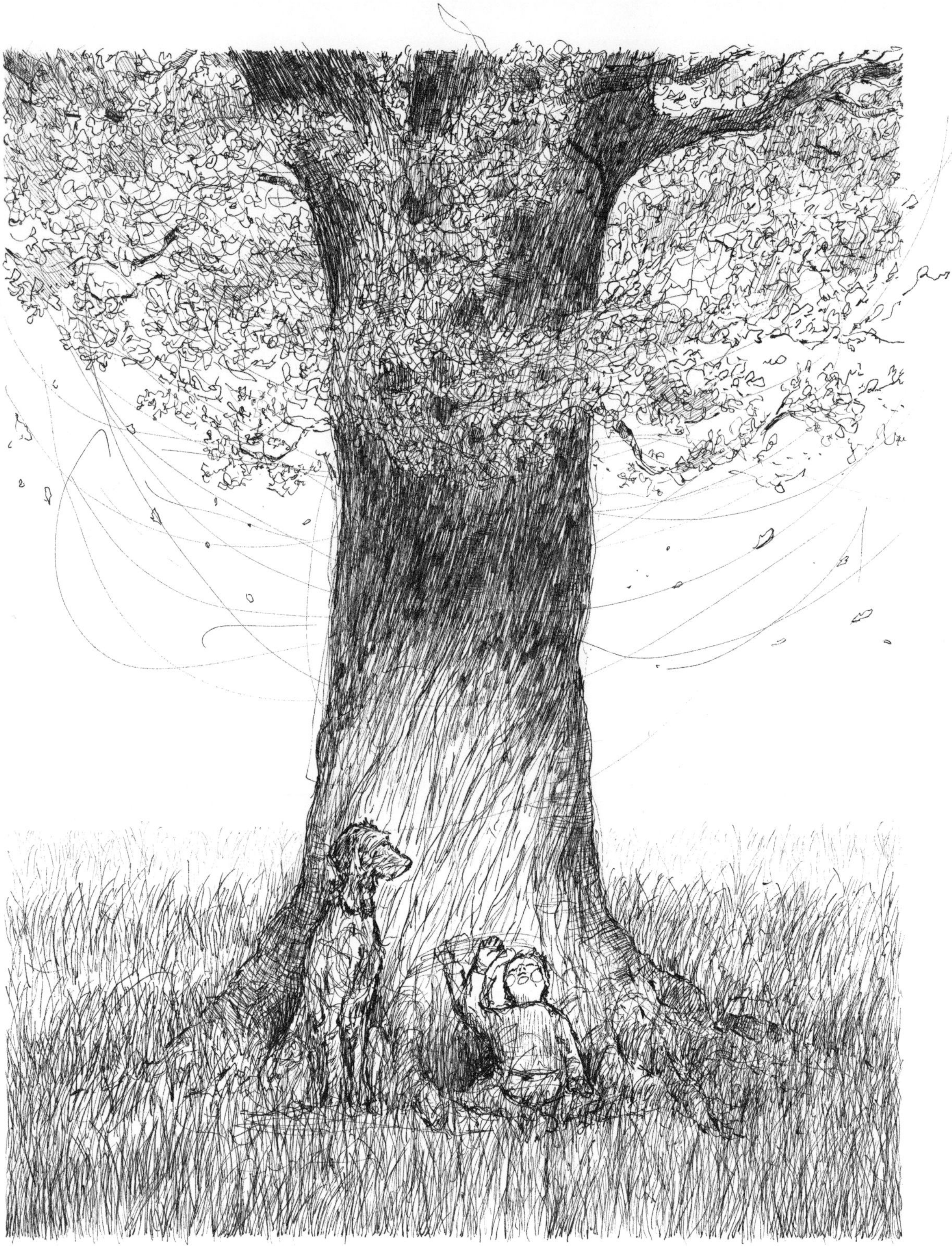

You found peace among the trees.
Seeing them, and feeling seen in return.

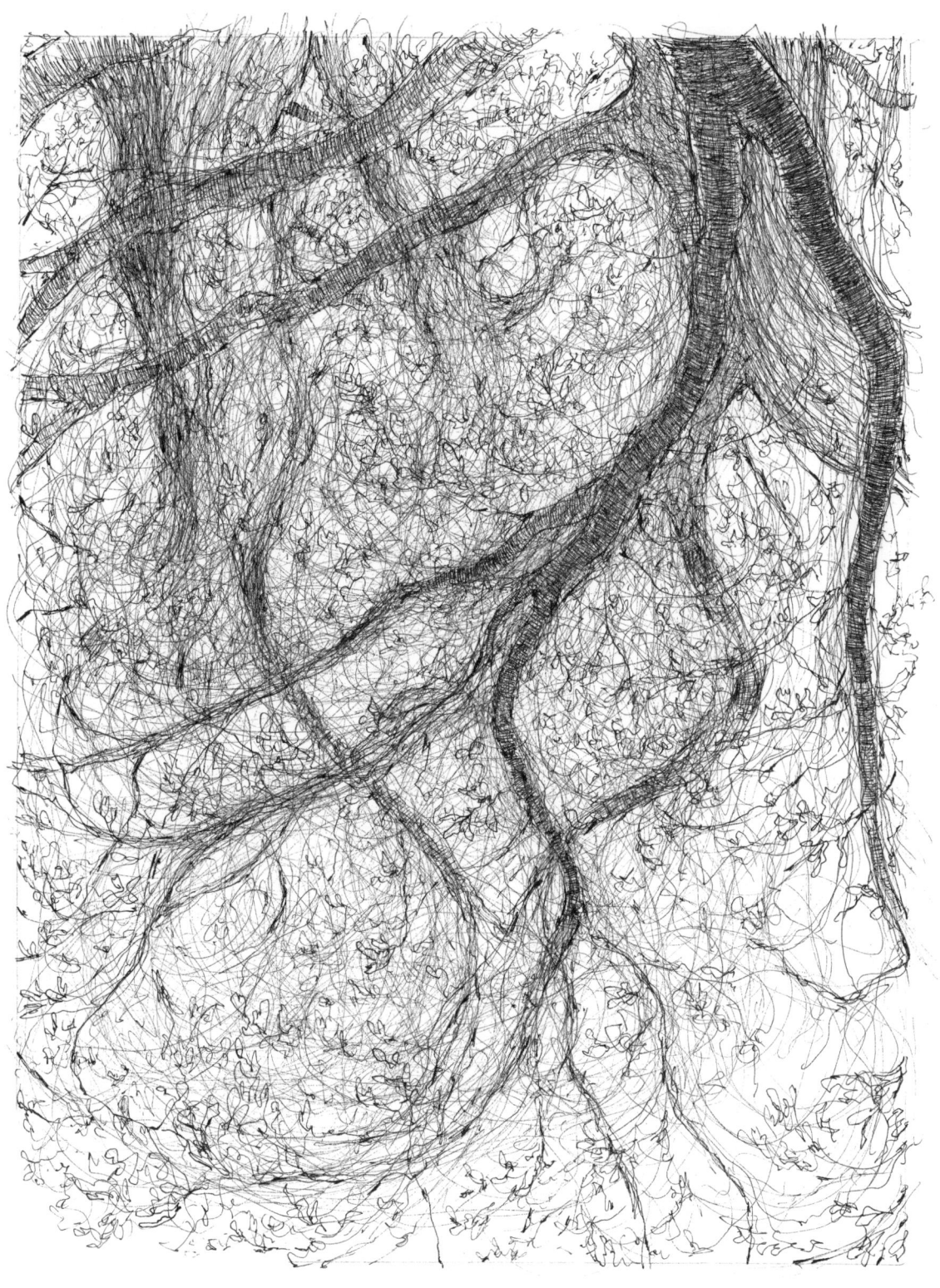

When the branches waved at you,
you never failed to wave back.

You say so much without uttering a word.

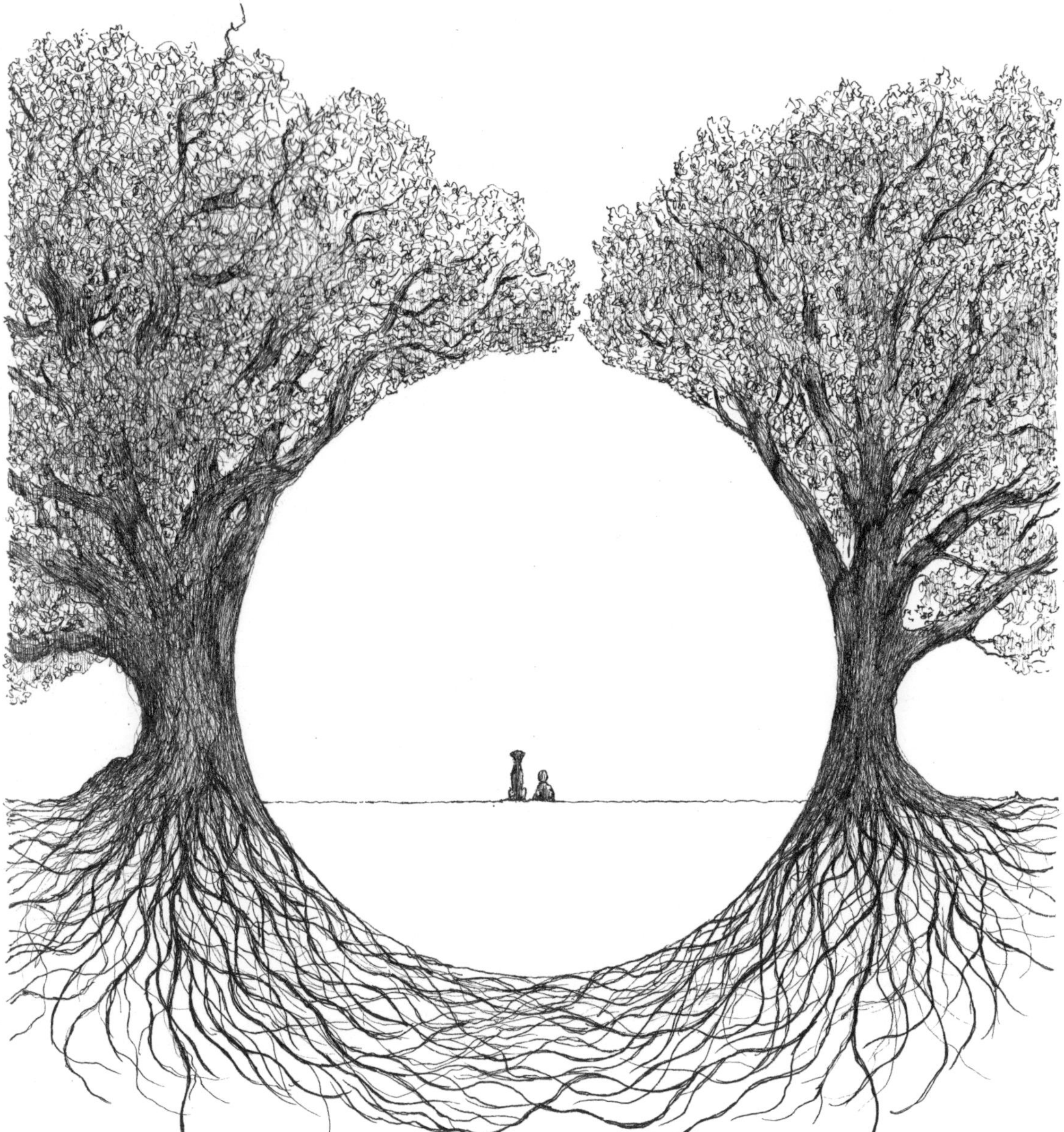

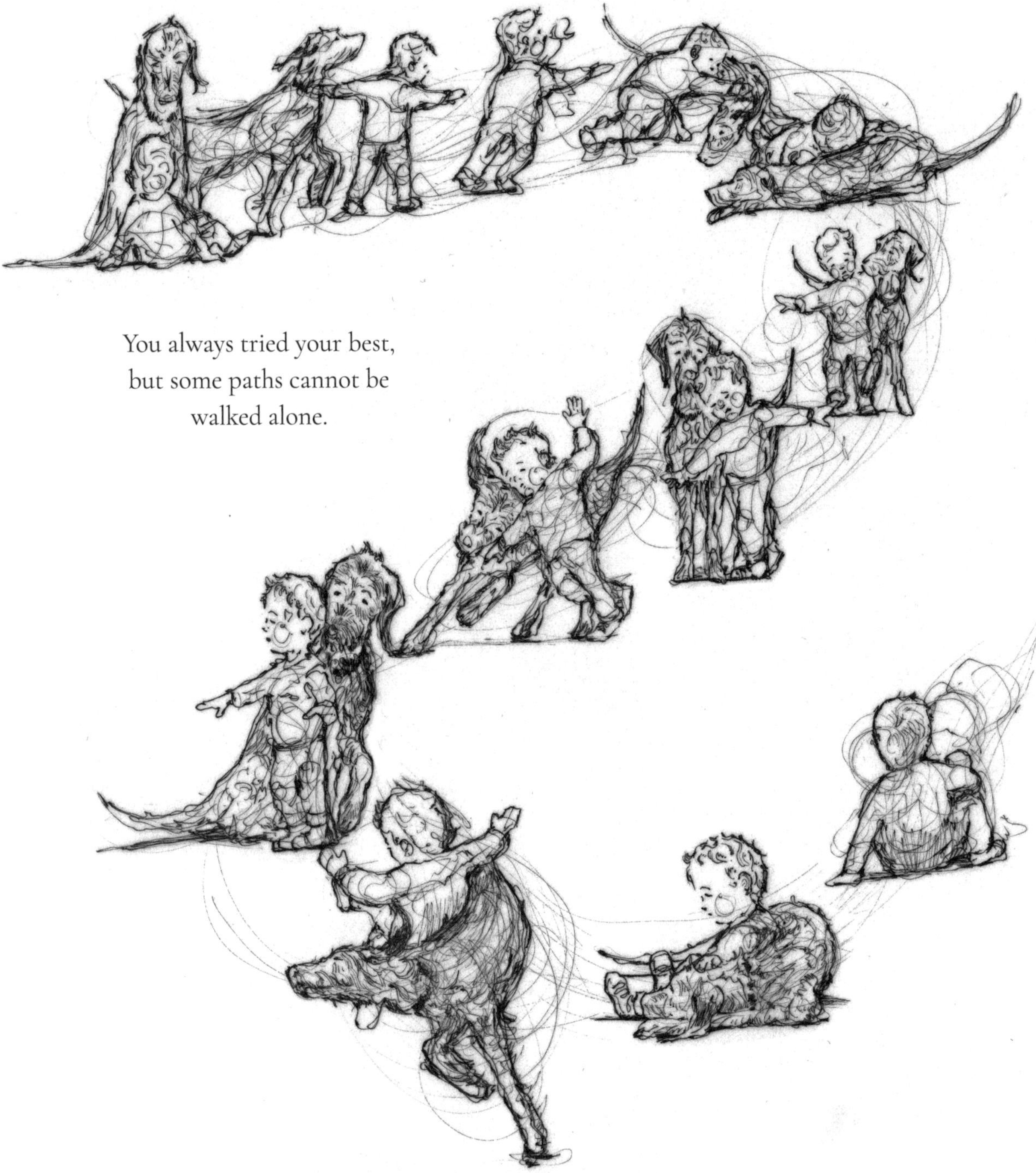

You always tried your best,
but some paths cannot be
walked alone.

So you walked together.

And made your own path.

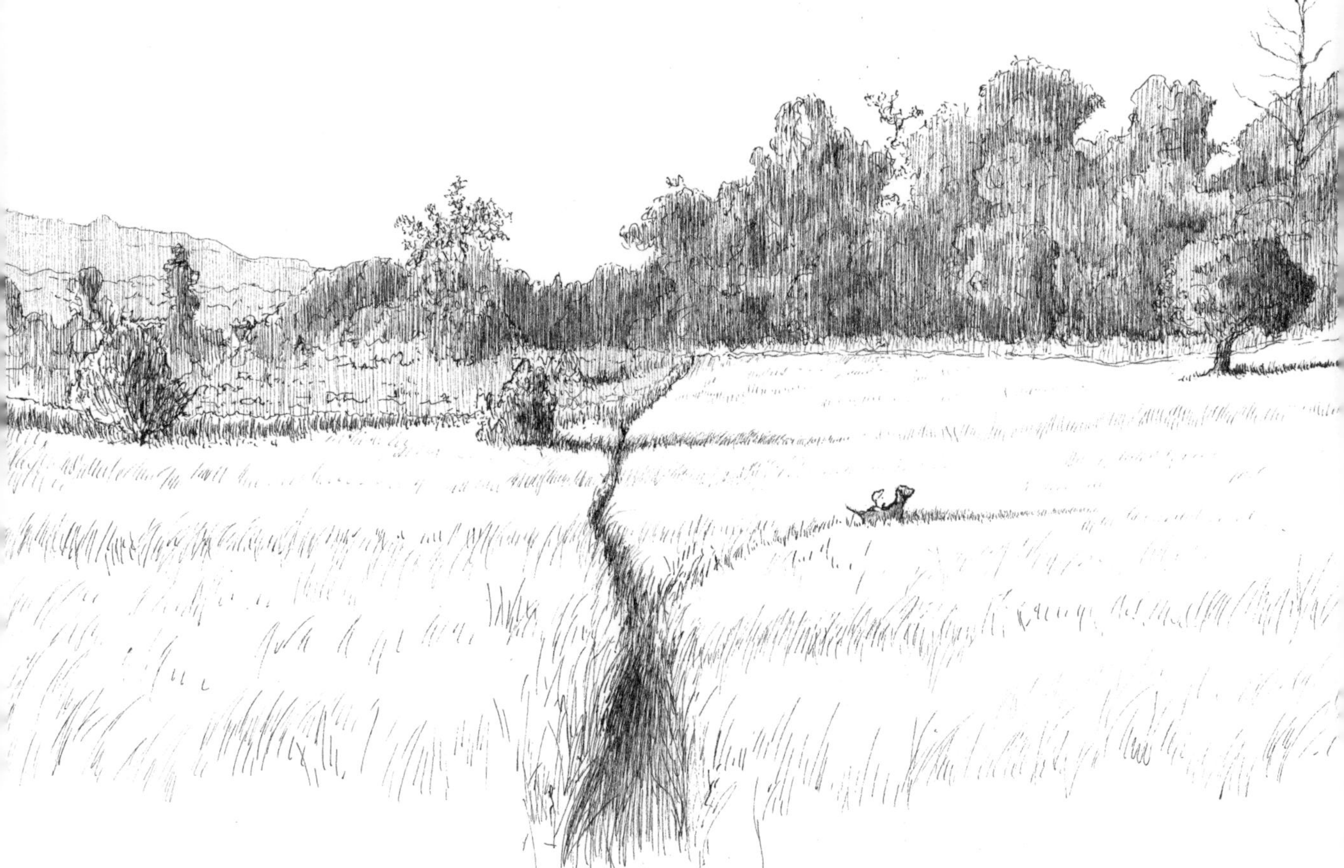

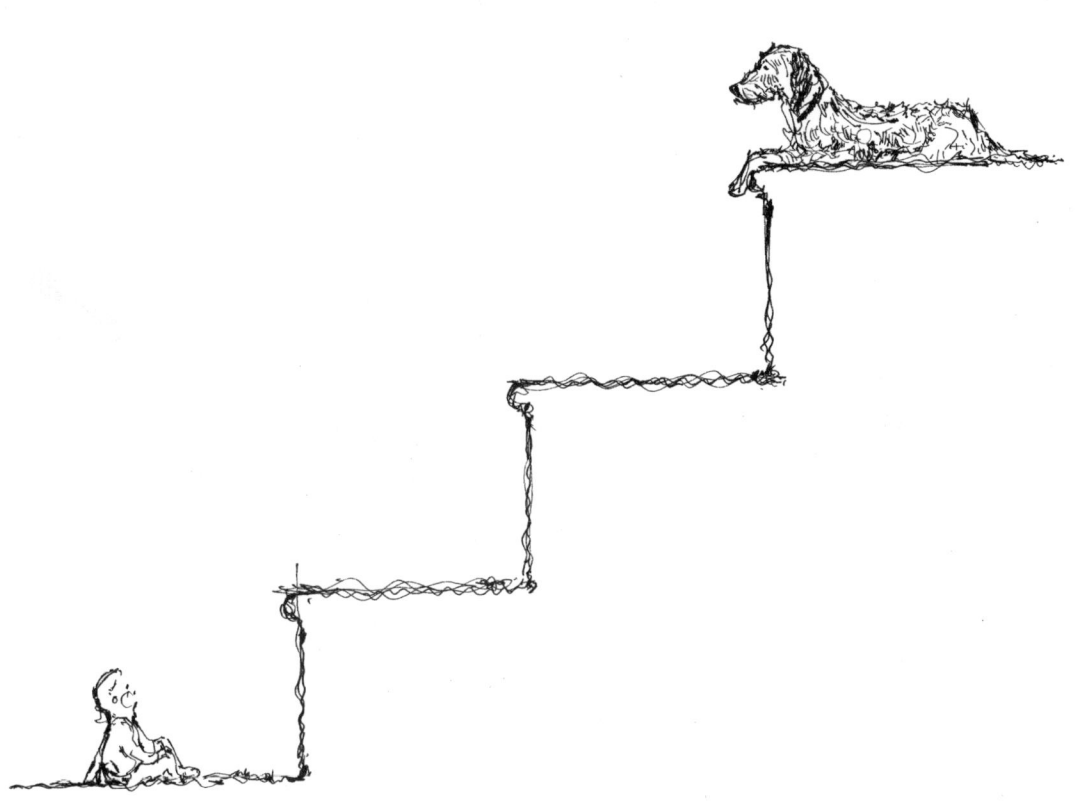

Forget milestones and tick-boxes.

Take it one step at a time.

You are exactly where you need to be.

Your first word was 'book', not spoken,
but shaped with your hands.

Beyond the pages of books,
this new language waited for you.

I used to wonder if you spoke in your dreams.
Now I know you sign.

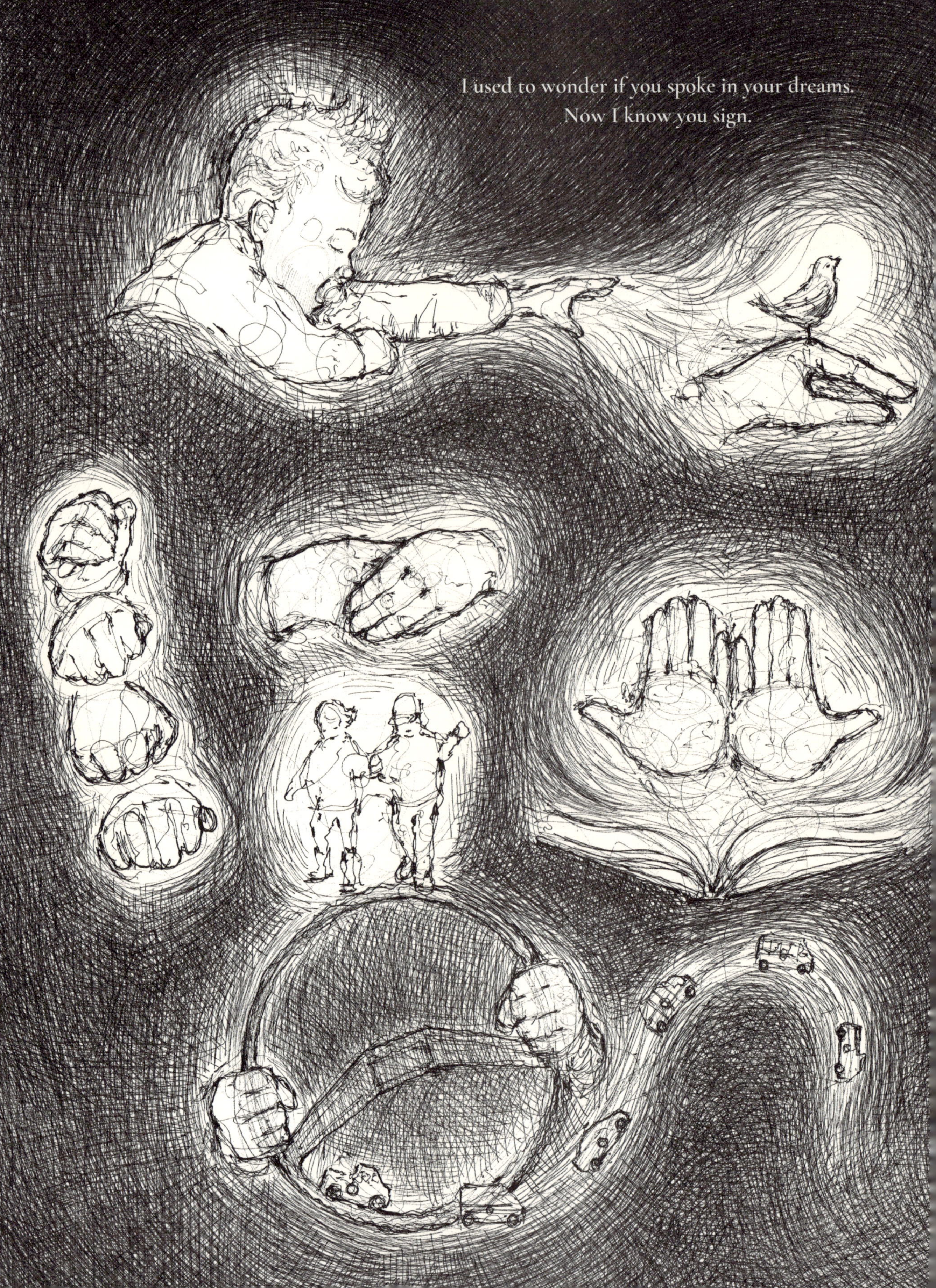

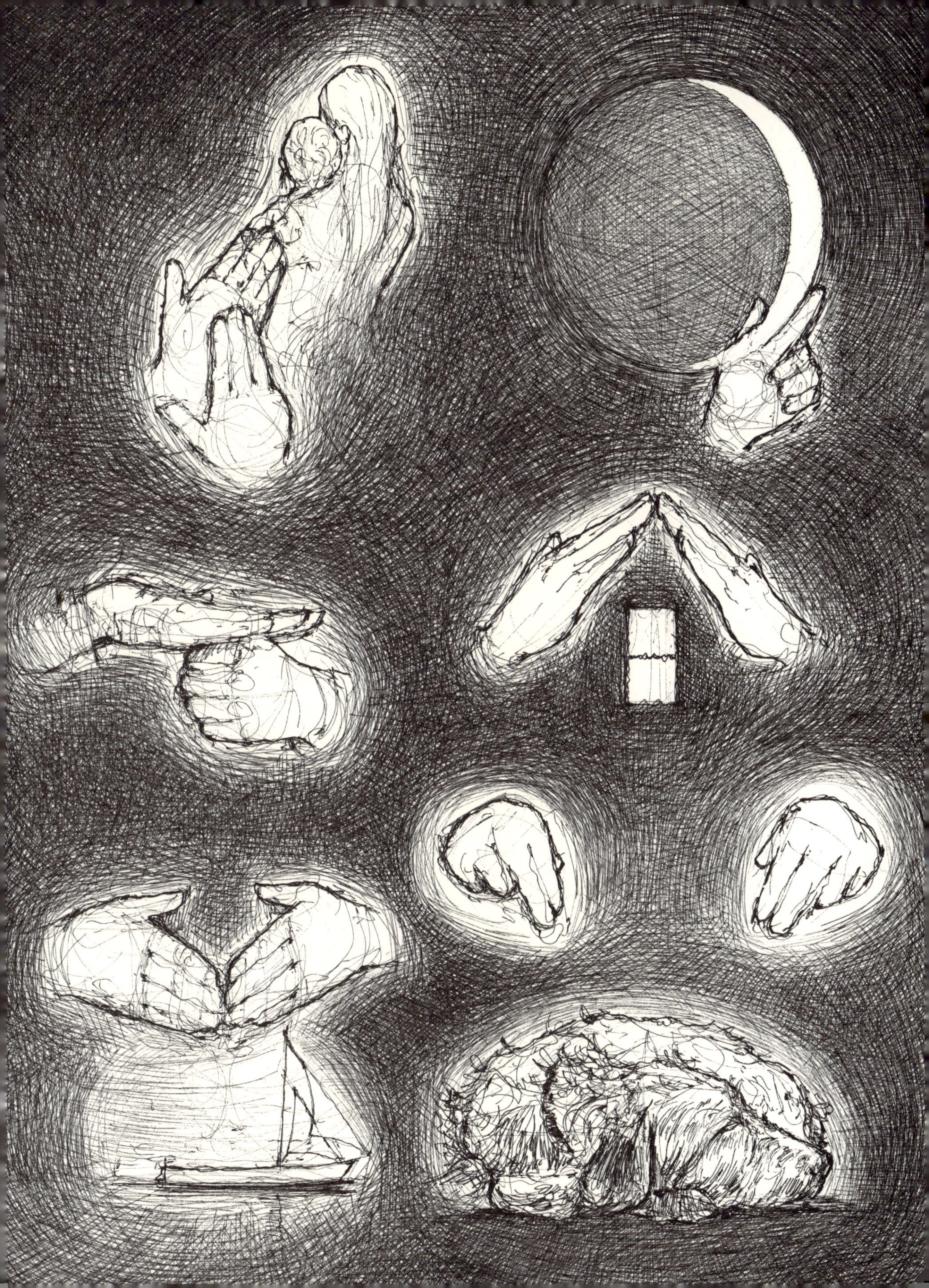

But dreams can quickly turn to nightmares.

You fell ill, needed help to breathe.

Your eyes said all we needed to know.

It was time to go.

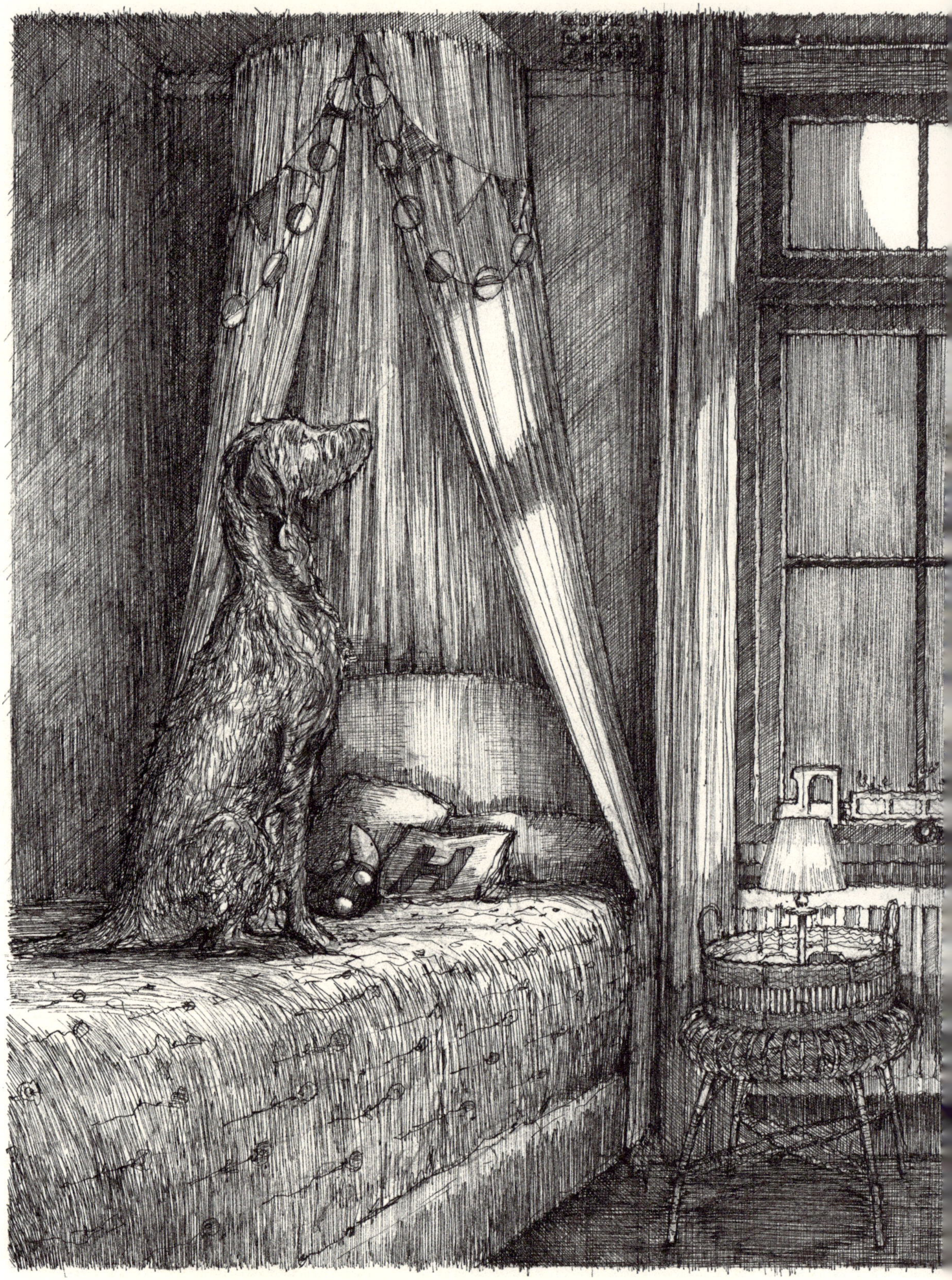

Separated, you longed for one another.

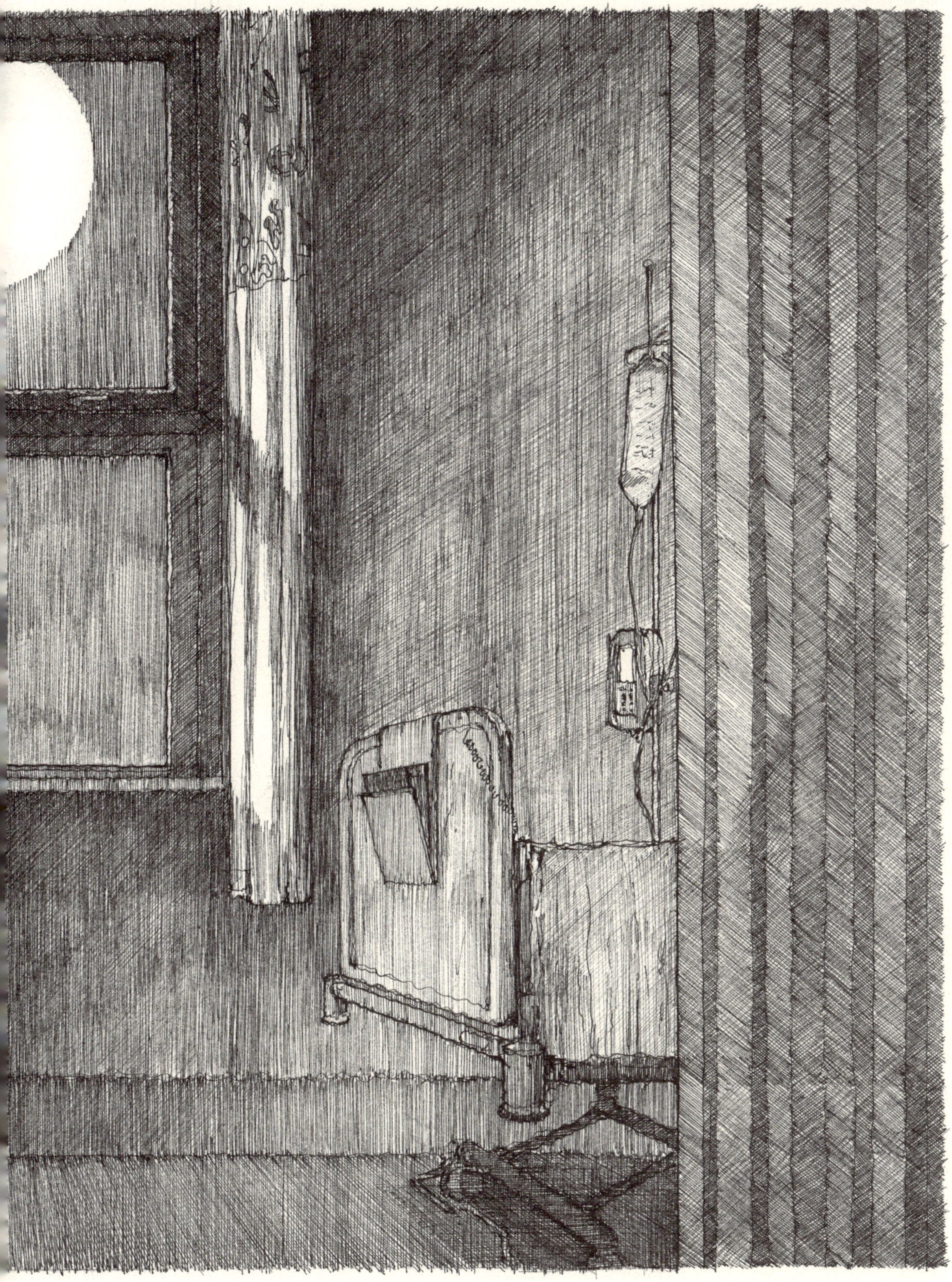

It was the best and the worst place to be.

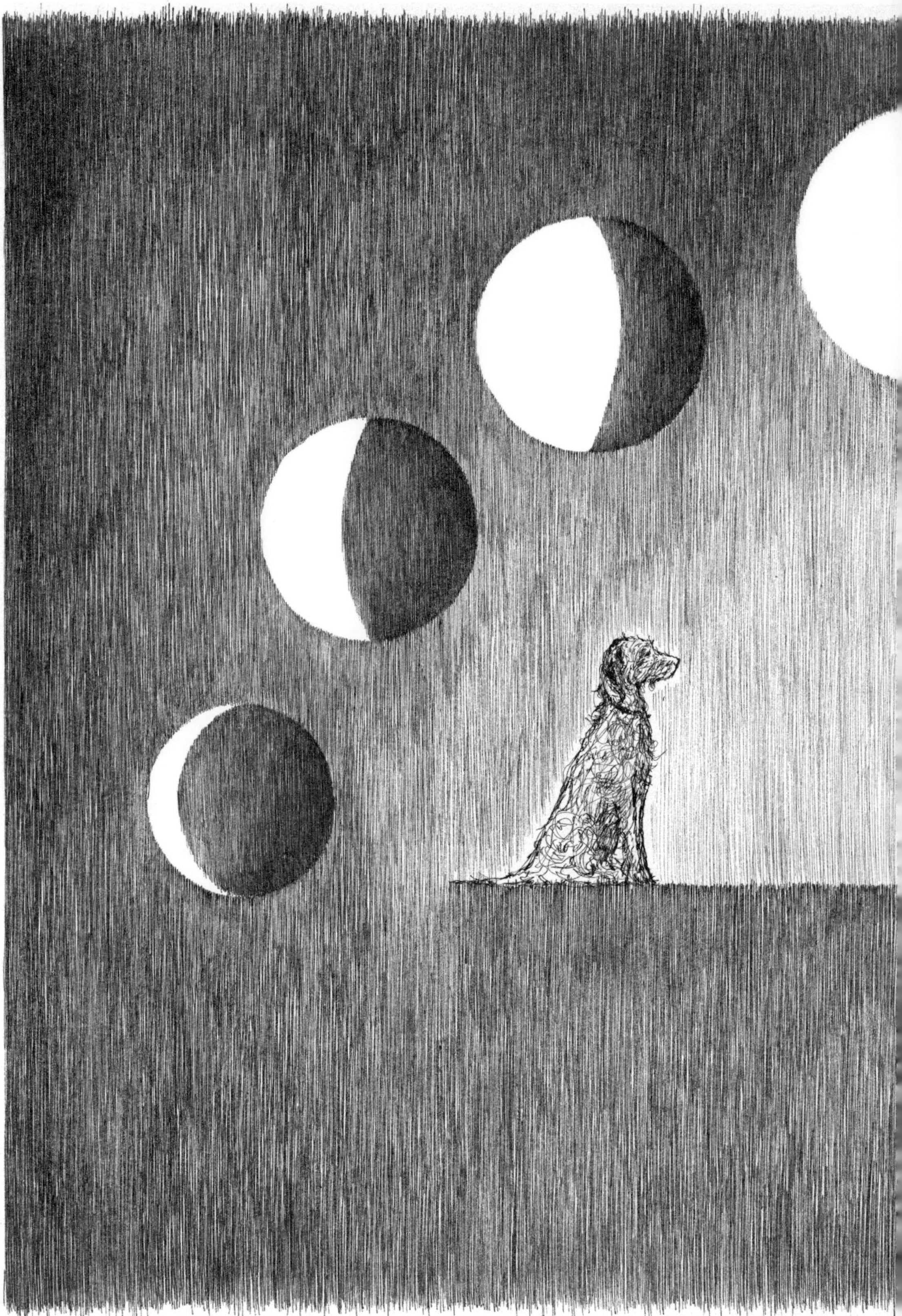

The nights were long.

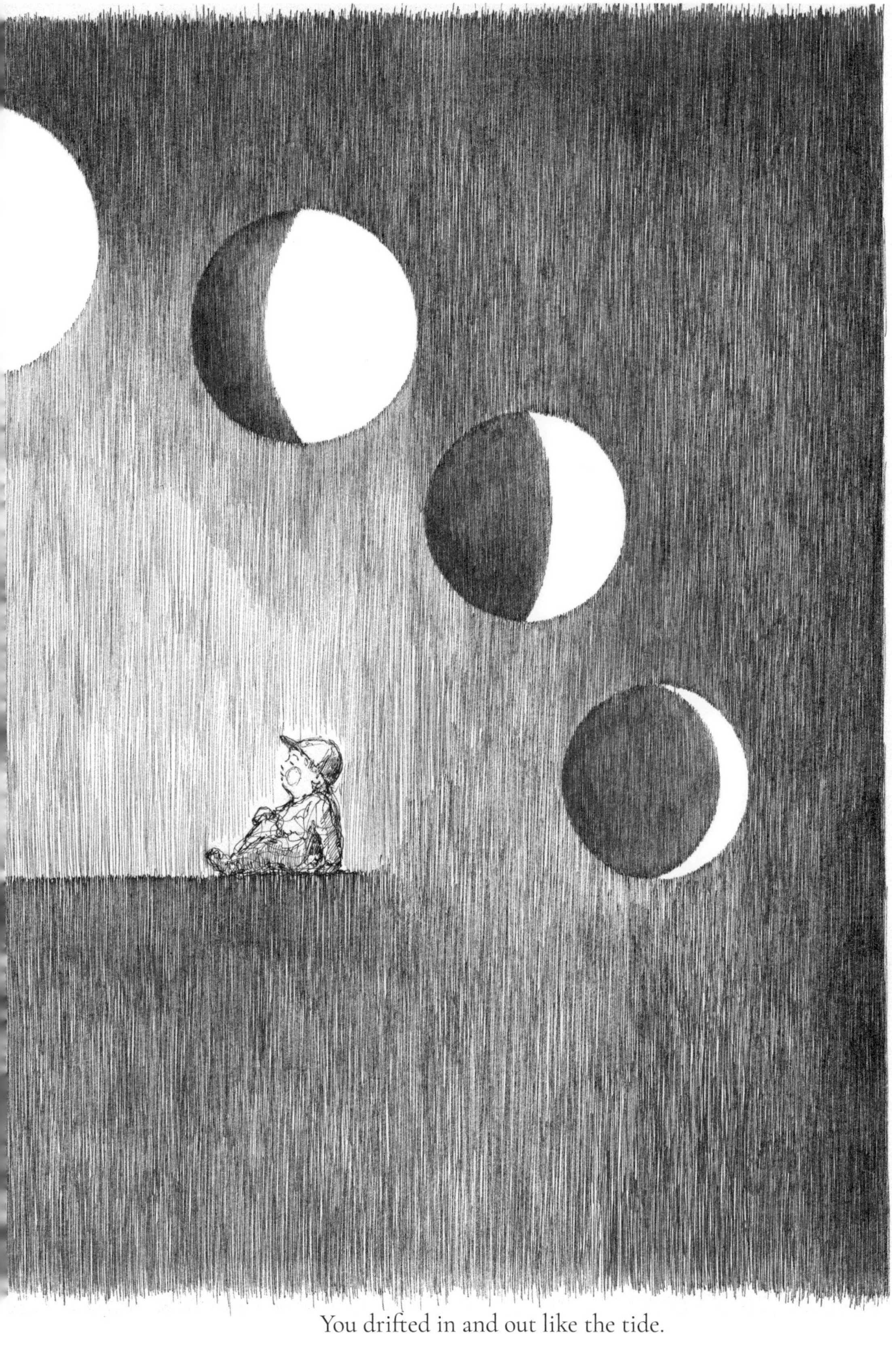

You drifted in and out like the tide.

Some bonds defy distance.

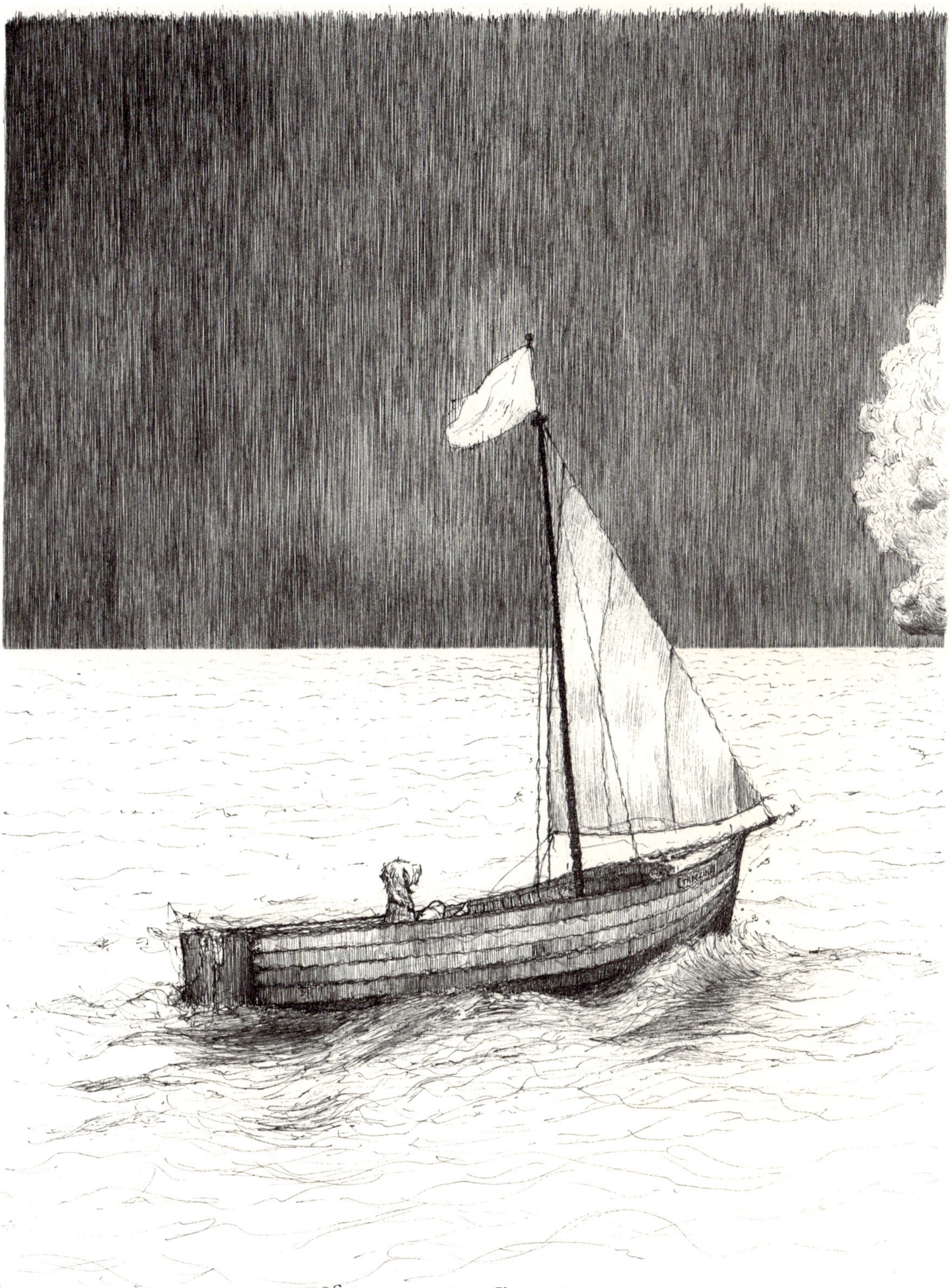

If you are going, I'm going too.
Wherever you go, I will follow.

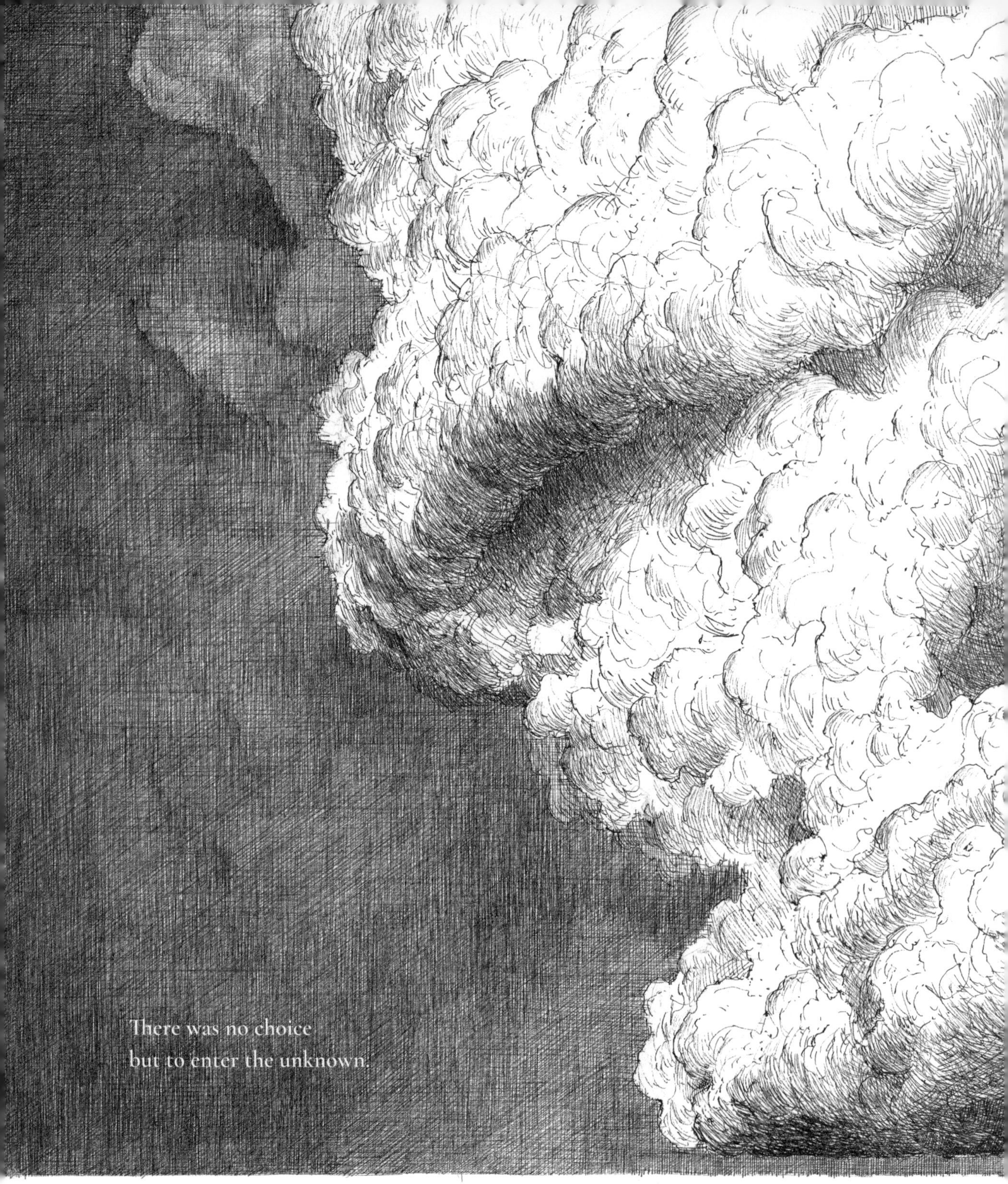

There was no choice
but to enter the unknown.

The only firm ground found in our embrace.

Contorted, distorted, curled into one.
You held on tight.

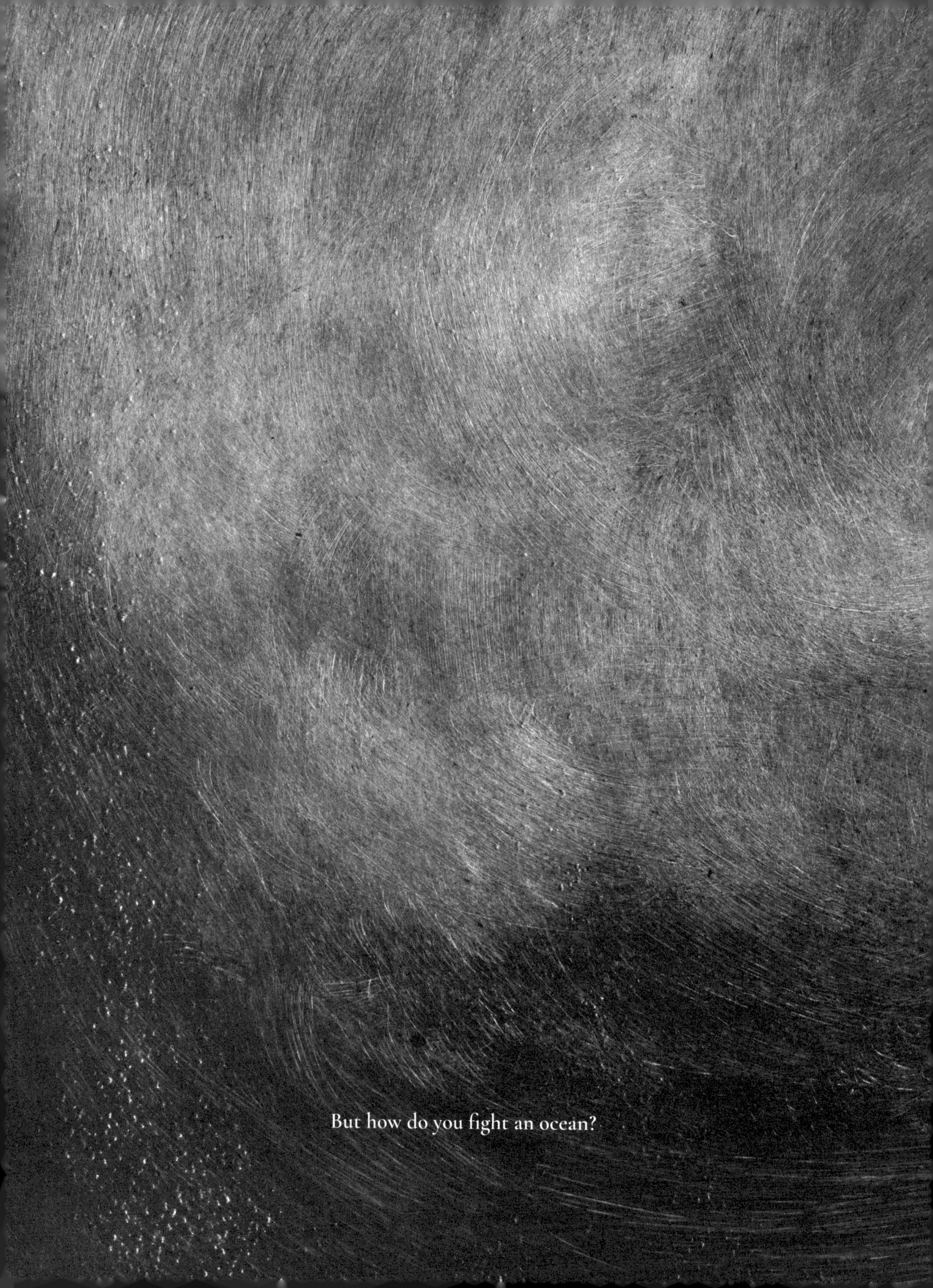

But how do you fight an ocean?

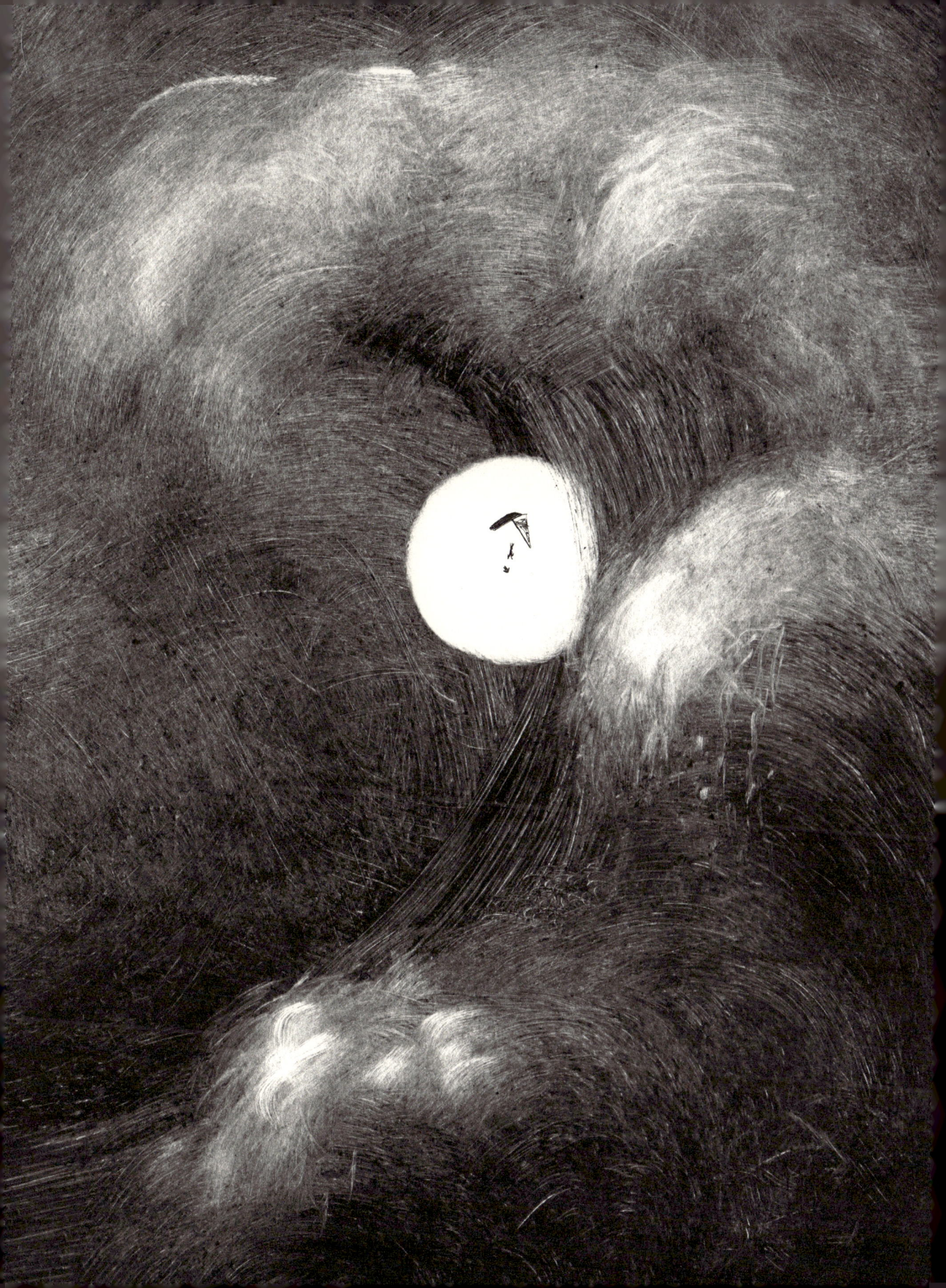

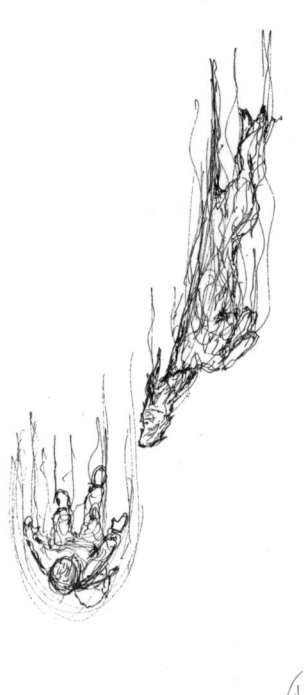

You were falling.

We longed to catch you.

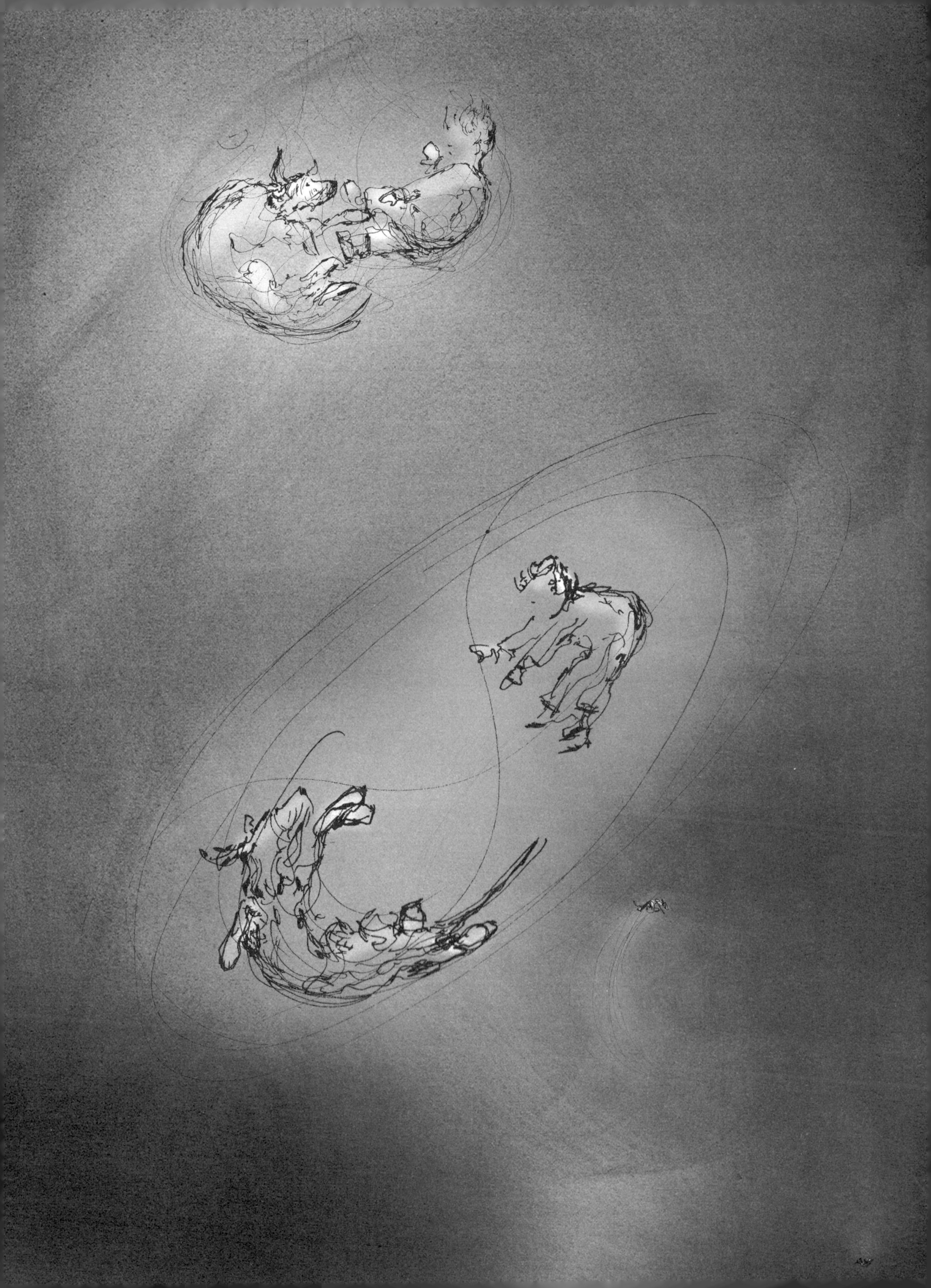

A sinking feeling.
Your breath shallow.

Your light never dimmed,
we just lost sight of it.

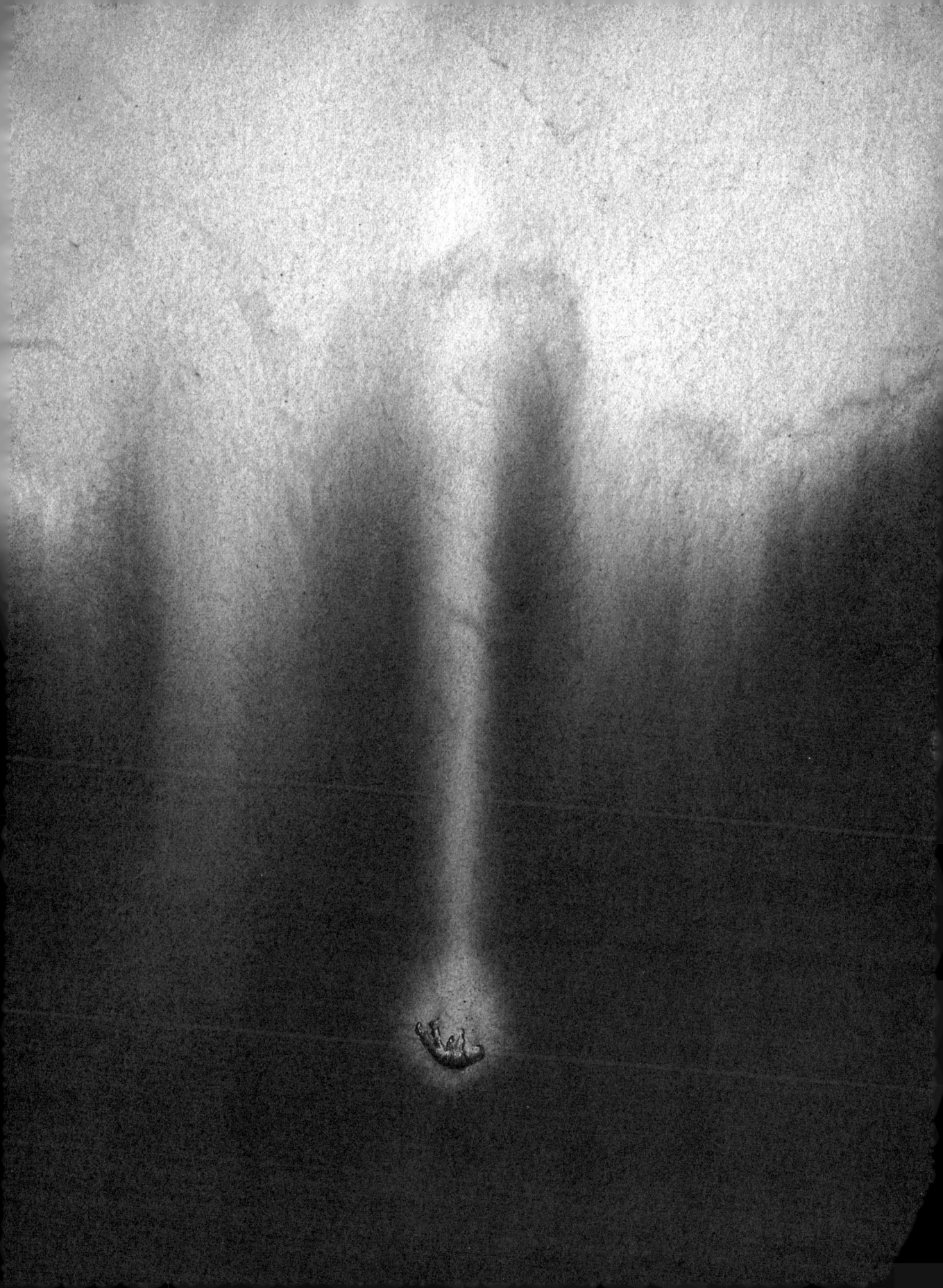

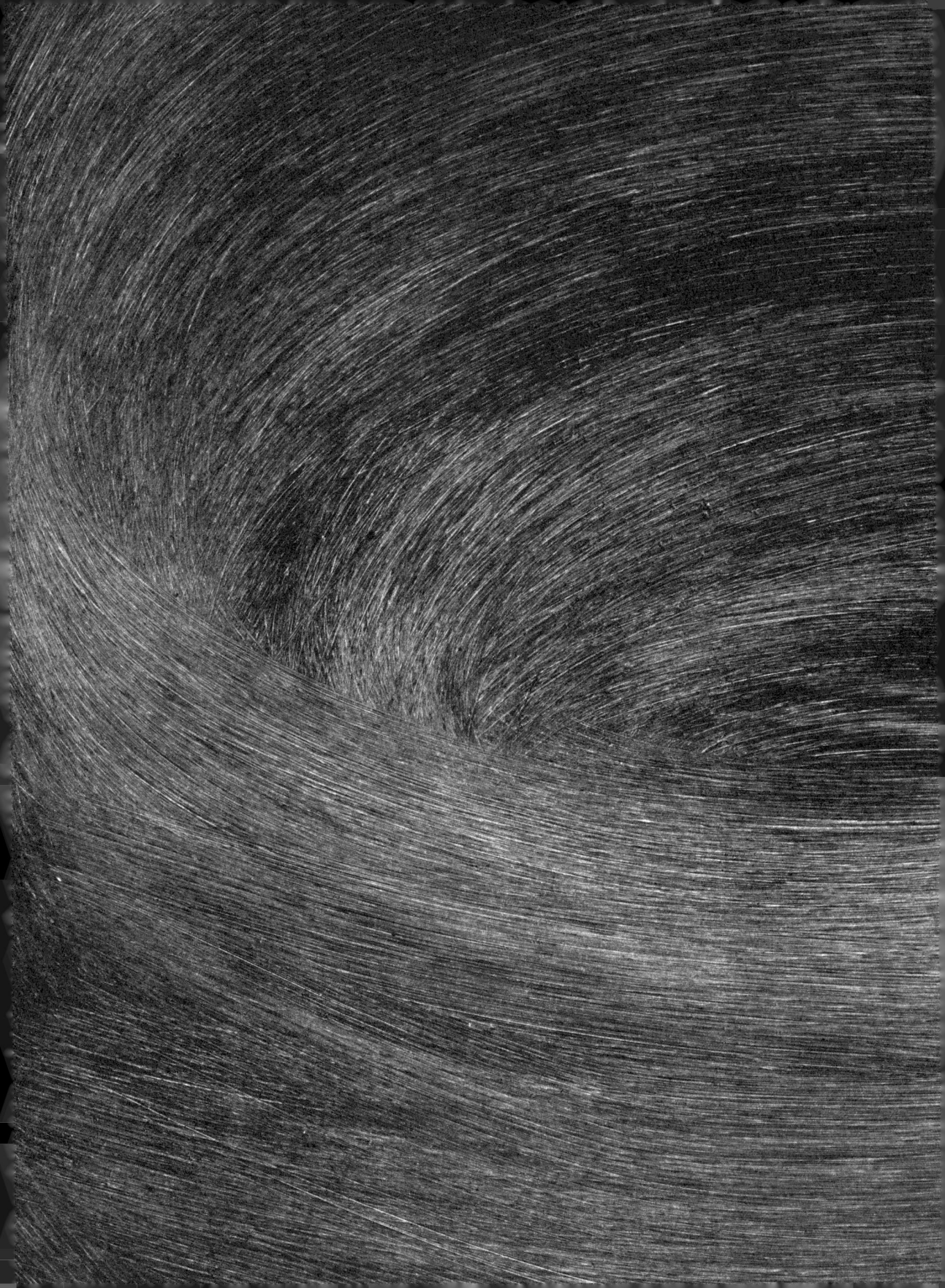

You went to a place we could not follow.
Time stood still.

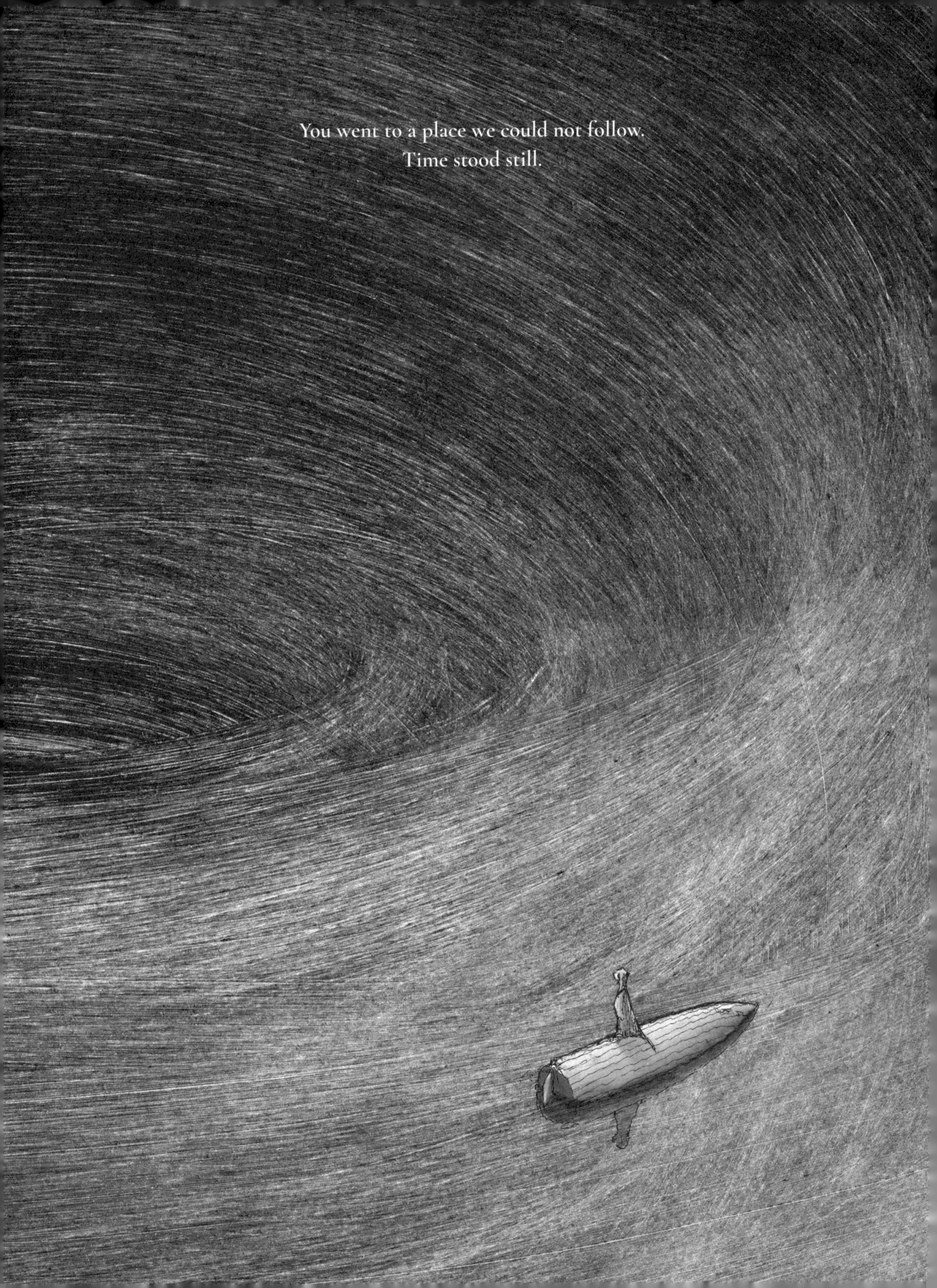

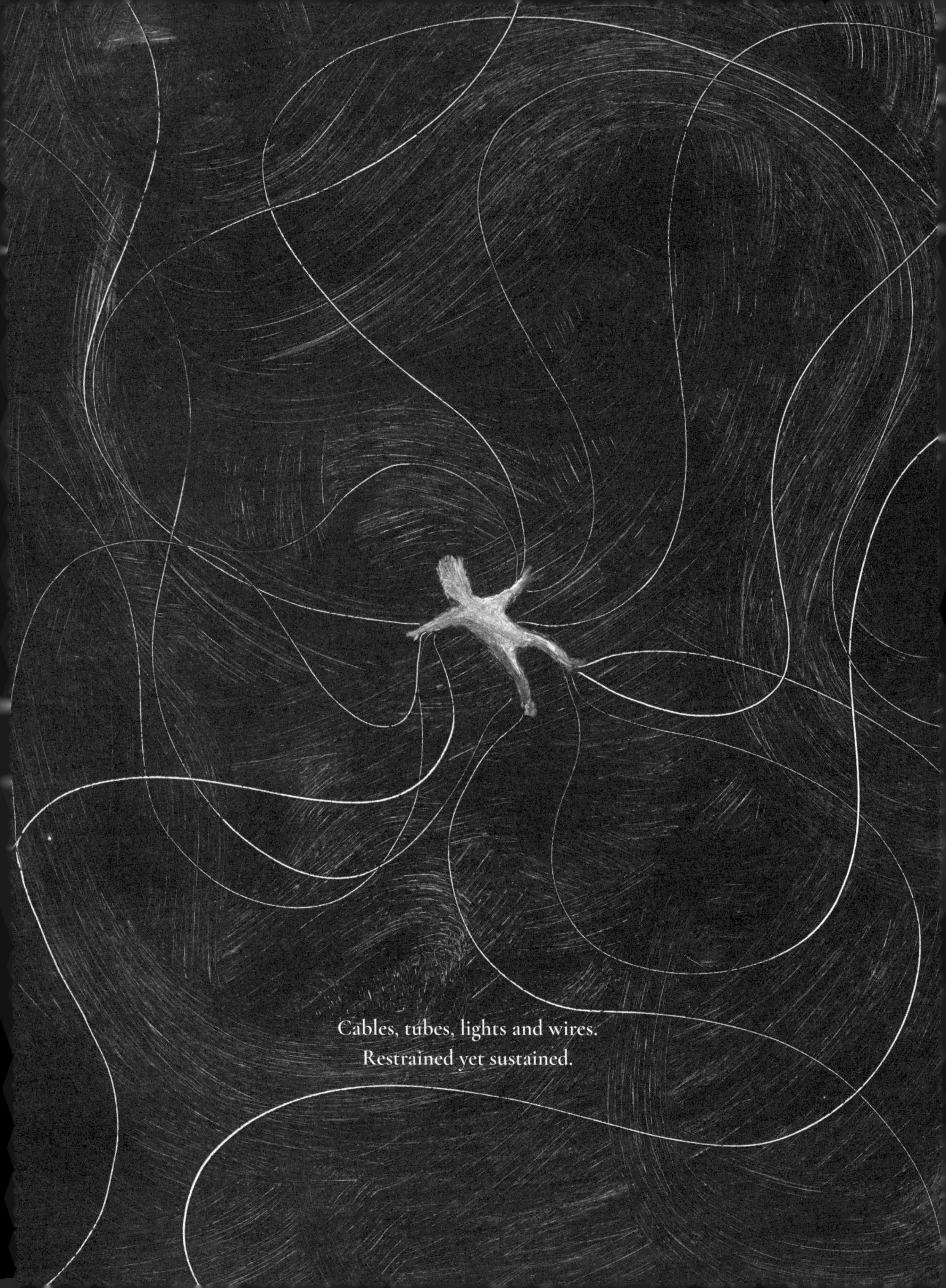

Cables, tubes, lights and wires.
Restrained yet sustained.

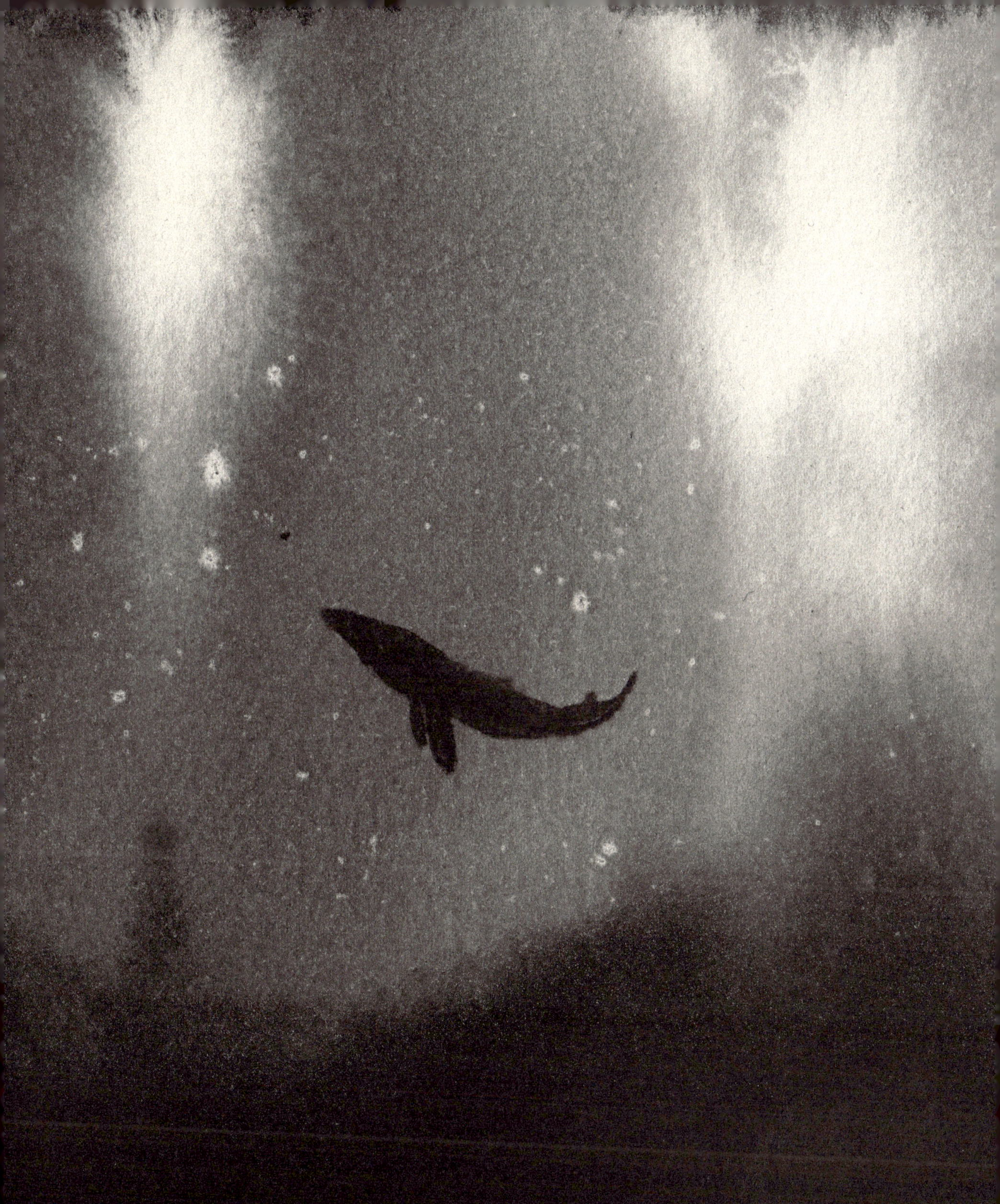

Thankfully, there are those who know how to navigate these depths

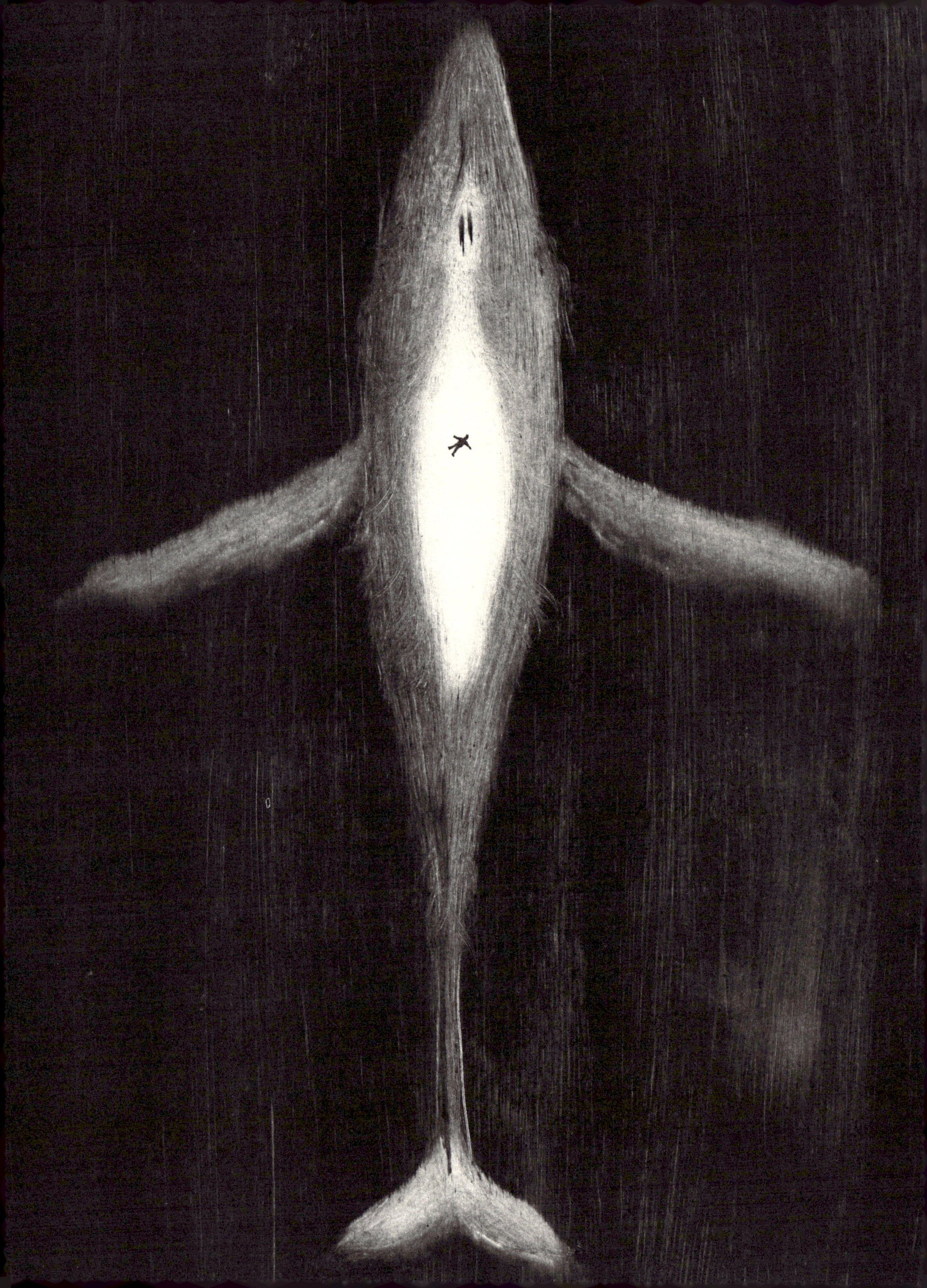

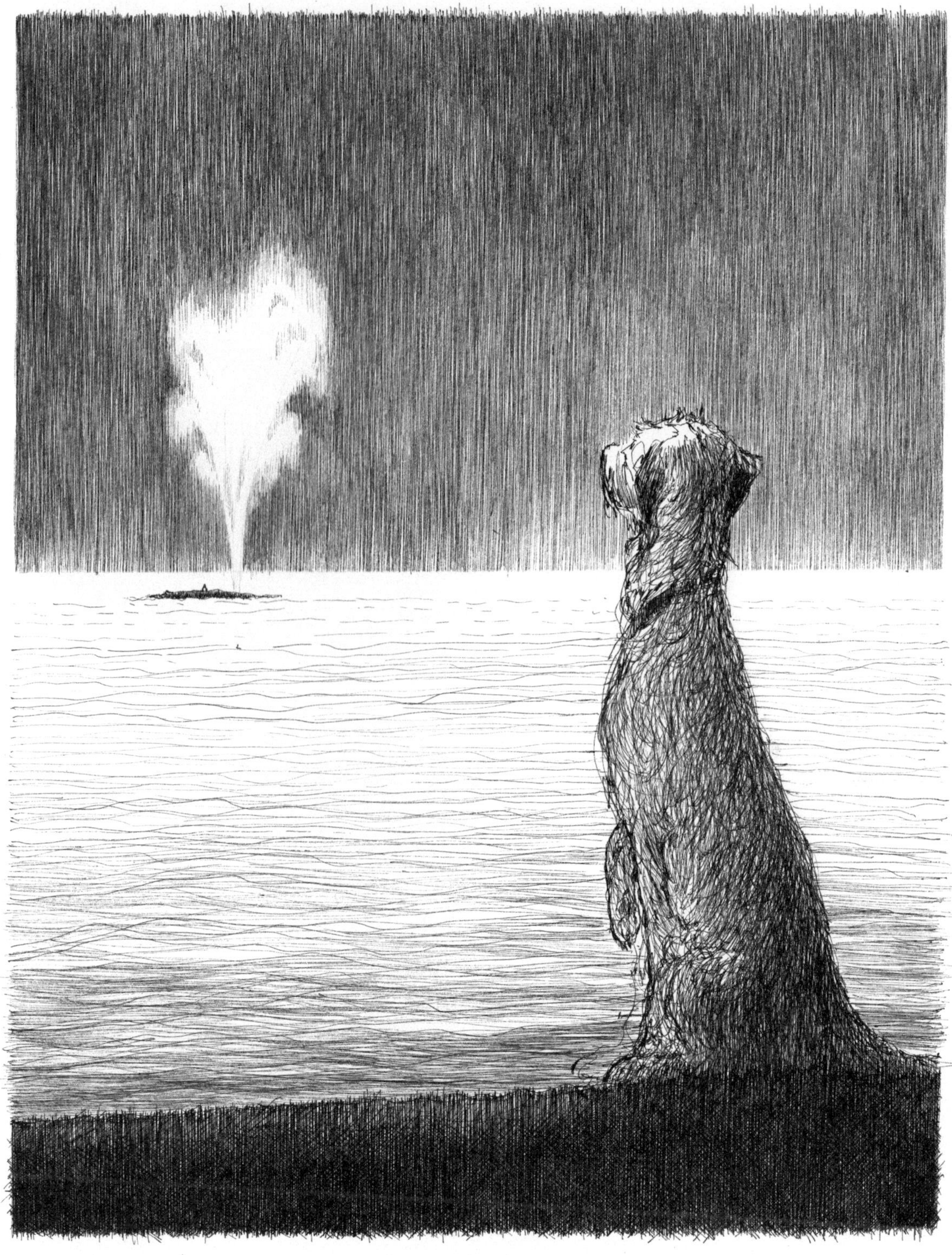

They brought you back to us.

And hope returned.

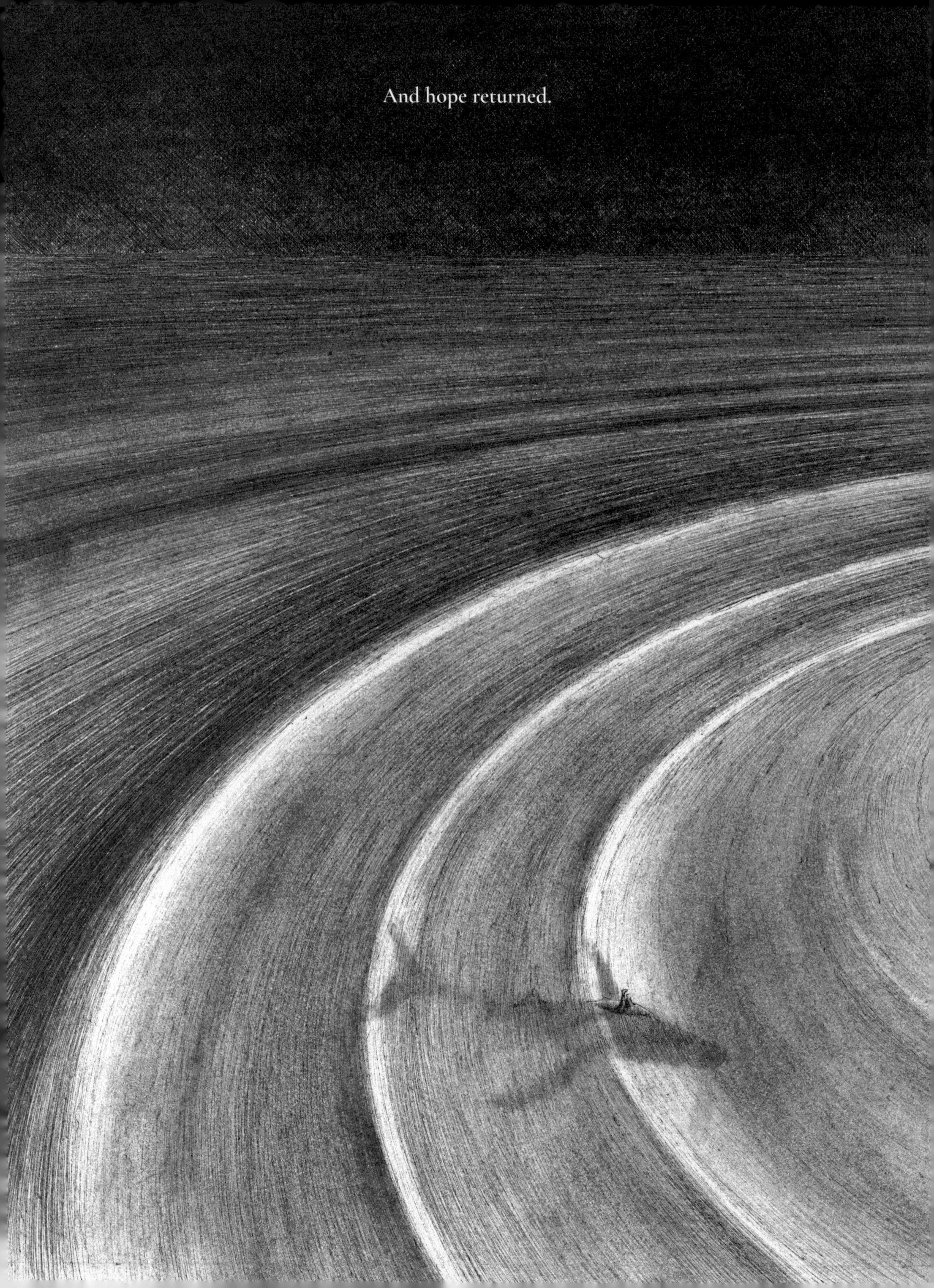

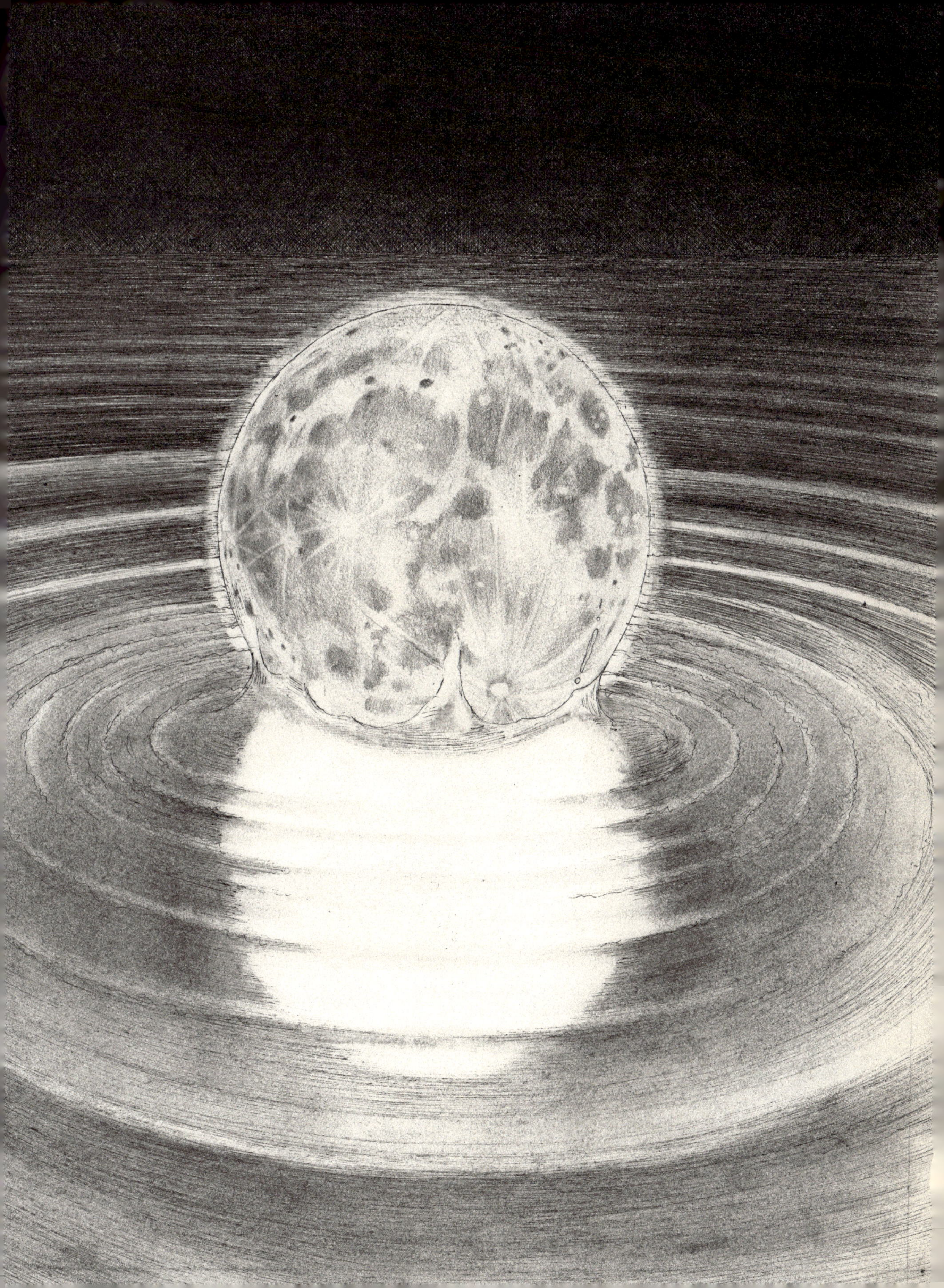

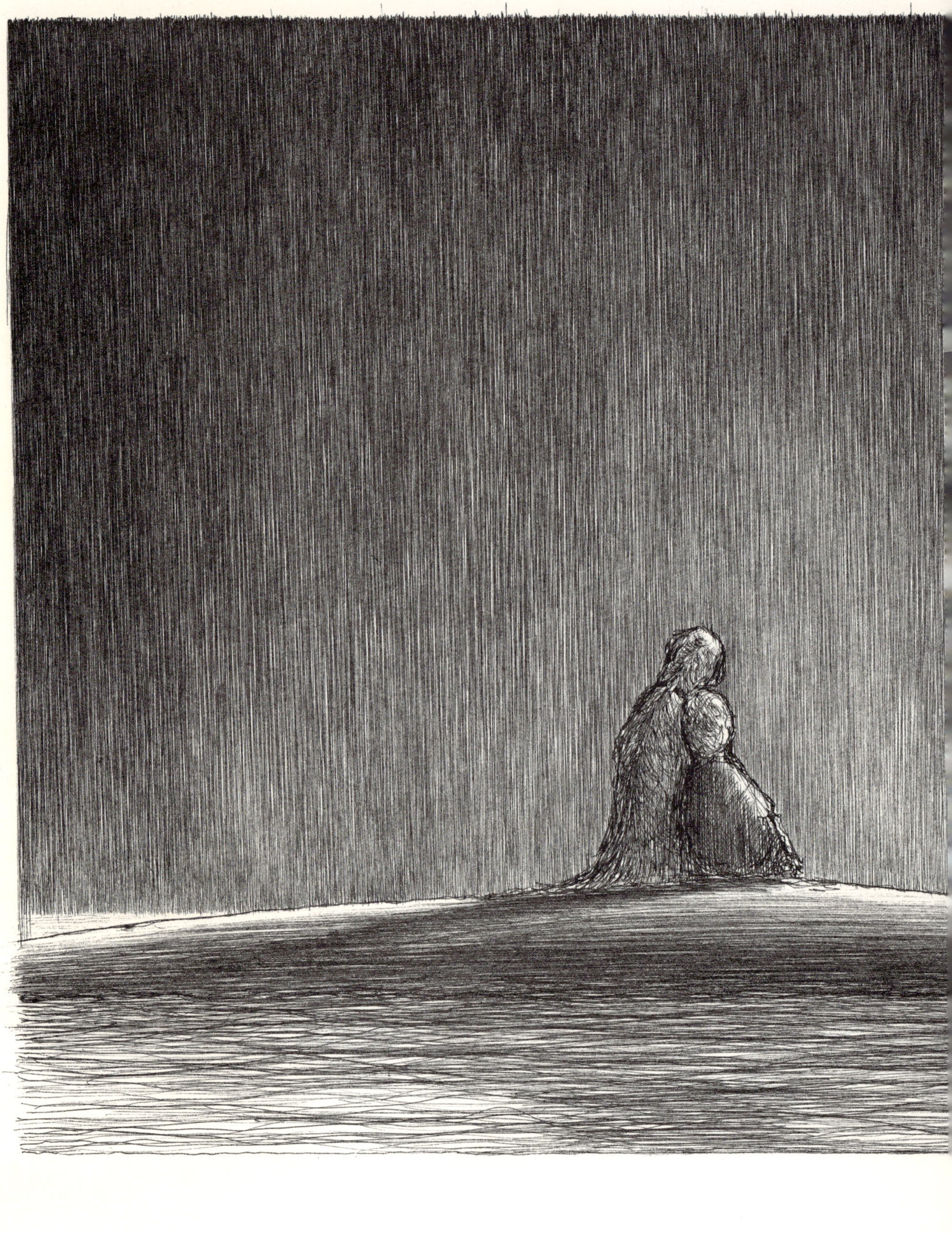

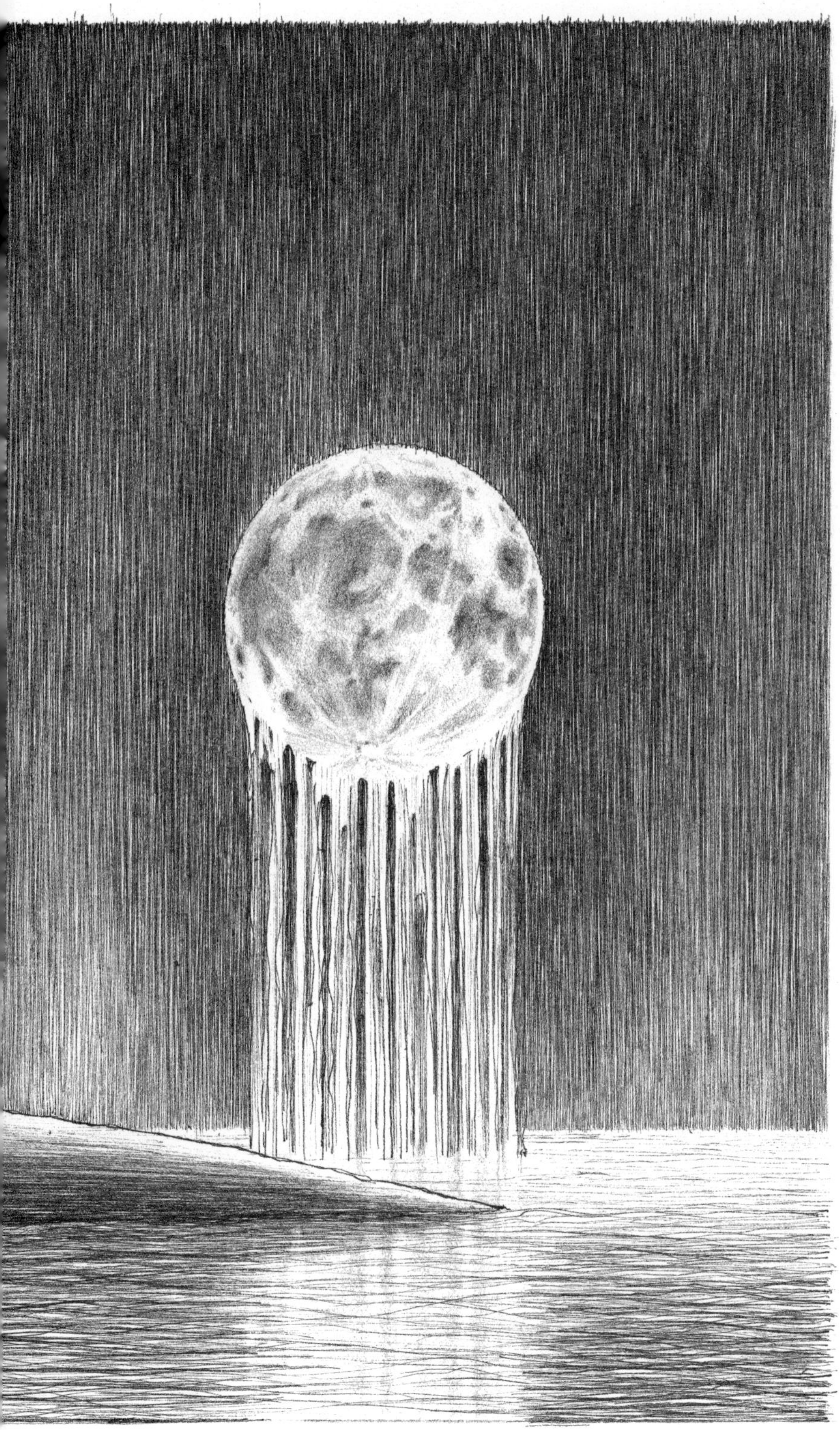

You were so weak
from your journey,
and yet still so
very strong.

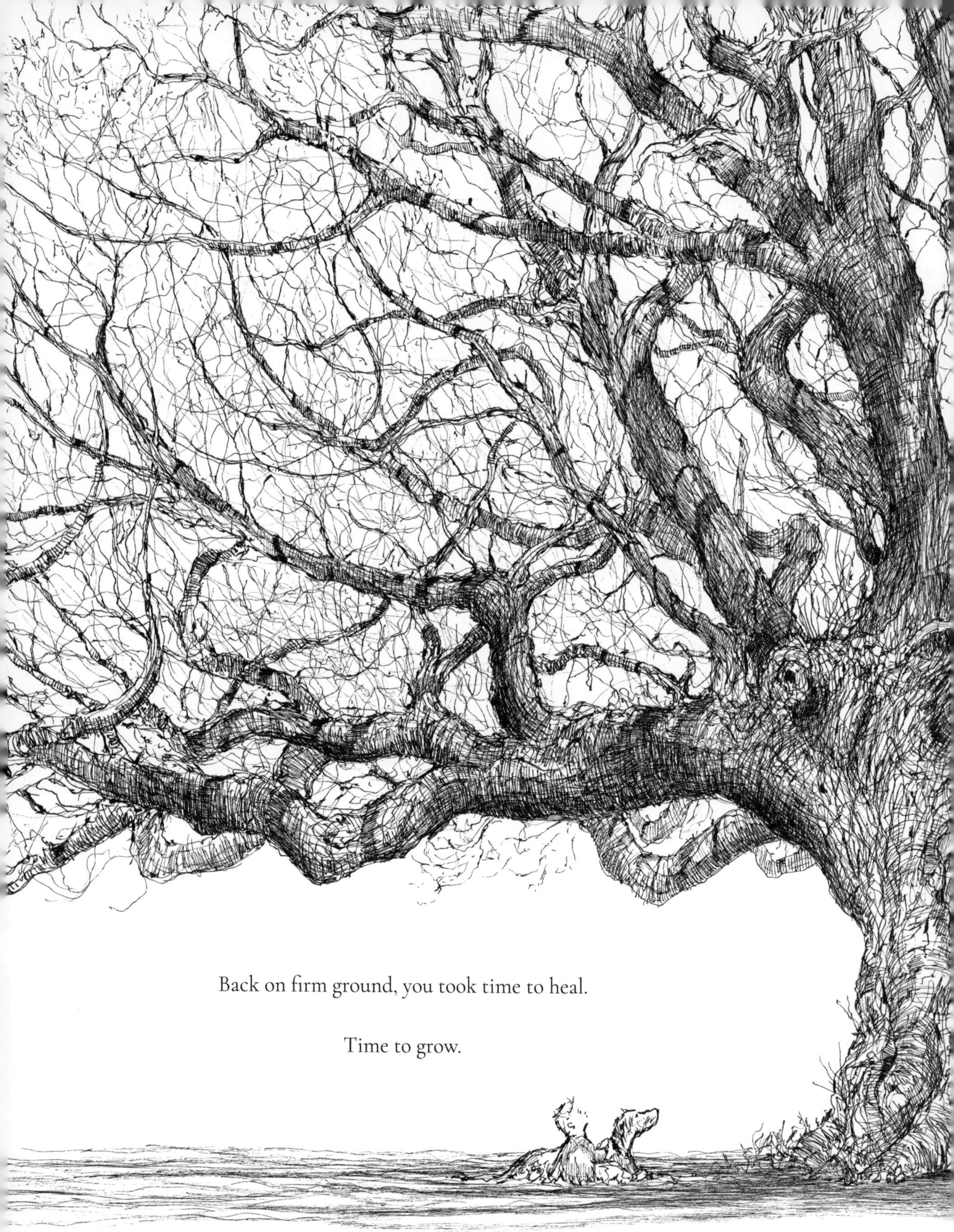

Back on firm ground, you took time to heal.

Time to grow.

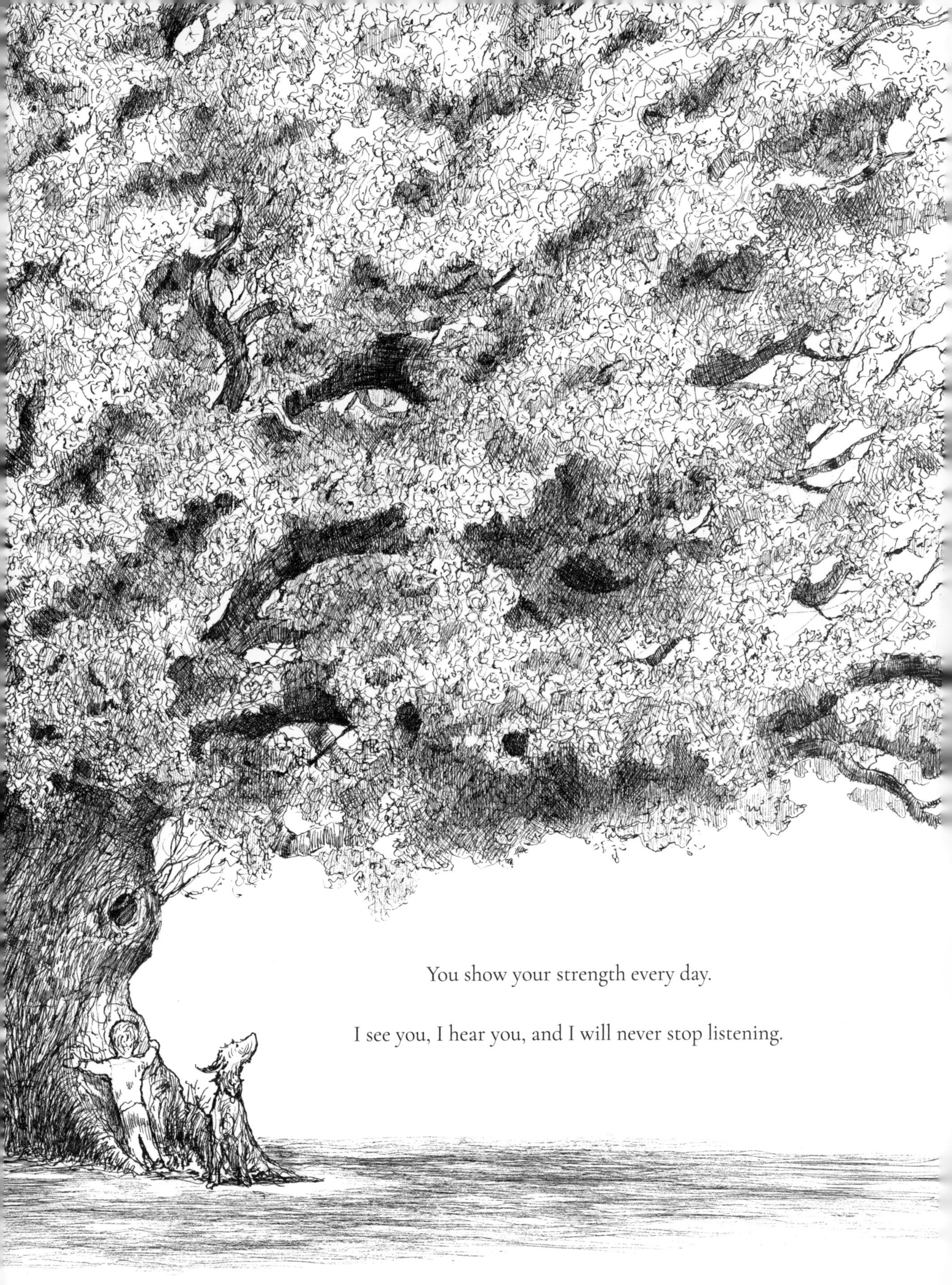

You show your strength every day.

I see you, I hear you, and I will never stop listening.

Keep being yourself, my son.

You are so very good at it.

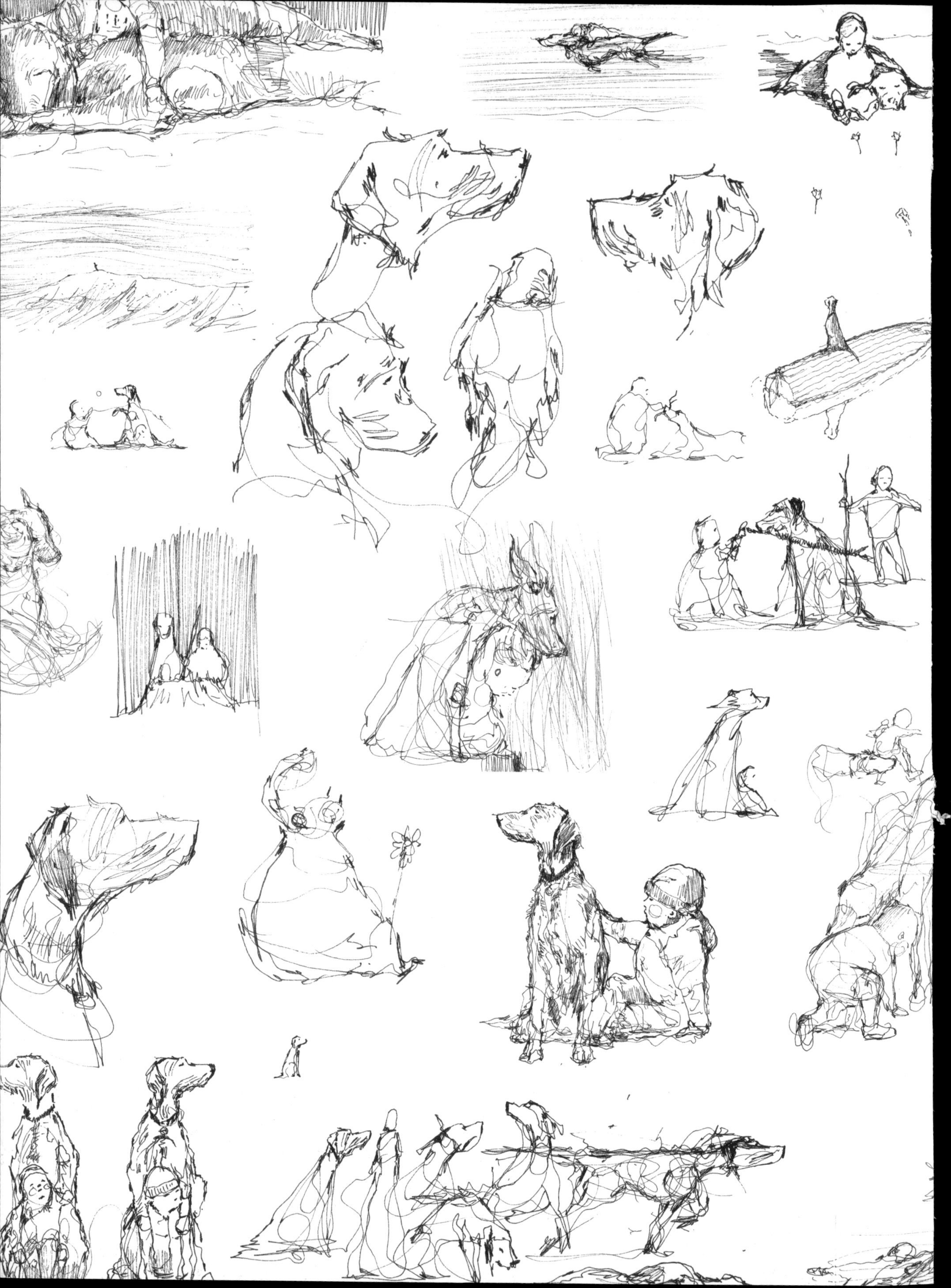